WE ARE ALL STAKEHOLDERS

SHIREEN MUHIUDEEN

WE ARE ALL Stakeholders

Culture, Politics,
AND
Radical Accountability
IN THE
Boardroom

CORSTON—SMITH®
ASSET MANAGEMENT

COPYRIGHT © 2023 SHIREEN MUHIUDEEN
All rights reserved.

WE ARE ALL STAKEHOLDERS
Culture, Politics, and Radical Accountability in the Boardroom

FIRST EDITION

ISBN   978-1-5445-3698-9   *Hardcover*
          978-1-5445-3699-6   *Paperback*
          978-1-5445-3700-9   *Ebook*

Dedicated to my late mum, Dr. Gwendolen Daisy Smith, an international pioneer for female physicians who dedicated her life to caring for children and other vulnerable, underserved populations. May my words and actions honor her uncompromising integrity, with hopes for a more sustainable, cooperative world.

CONTENTS

INTRODUCTION

Rather than a shattered glass ceiling, my ascent to the boardroom brought me face-to-face with massive, floor-to-ceiling carved wooden doors: I was about to become the first woman to enter that room as a director.

Typically the boardroom occupies the highest story of a corporate building—and for good reason. These imposing doors represent entry to the pinnacle of corporate leadership. Not in terms of status or perks, but in terms of impact—and no, I'm not just talking about a company's bottom line.

At these heights, the view may seem grand, but the stakes can be dizzying.

Discussions that take place on the other side of doors like these may well determine whether or not the Earth dangerously—and irreparably—overheats. Corporate board decisions have a direct and lasting effect on everything from global digital security to human trafficking to plastic waste. They trickle down to every level of a company, across our communities, and into our homes.

Considering the reach and weight of boardroom deliberations, a newcomer might expect a solemn tone within its walls—approximating perhaps the reverent hush of a library, or formal dignity of a courtroom. Nothing could prepare me for the pandemonium I found instead.

THROUGH THE BOARDROOM DOORS

To be fair, my initiation to the world of the publicly listed boardroom was an ad hoc meeting, called to address the urgent matter of company cargo ships—or rather, one particular ship hauling combustible materials that had caught fire just offshore from a heavily populated Asia-Pacific coastline. It seemed clear to me that, as company leaders, we needed to immediately halt and evacuate the burning ship offshore to prevent a potential explosion engulfing the shipping port and killing thousands of people.

While that is precisely what we did, it was hardly a foregone conclusion. Some voices in the room insisted we find a way to dock and salvage cargo, clearly willing to risk a potential catastrophic loss of human life for short term ROI.

We went on to discuss multiple fatalities resulting from a combination of newly purchased construction equipment and reduced safety training—a topic we would devote several more meetings to. Plus, we'd just received notice of a potential lawsuit regarding an internal matter. Far from the somber restraint of a courtroom, the scene swiftly devolved into curses, shouts, and worse. Let's just say that before that meeting adjourned, I watched as both threats and a piece of furniture got hurled across the room.

No stranger to the global marketplace, I wasn't surprised our agenda should (would) focus on worker safety, environmental hazards, and legal threats. Also not shocking: the observed reluctance to sacrifice profits in service to the greatest possible good for the Earth and humanity at large. I understood that international commerce relies on complex sociopolitical dynamics, shareholder obligations, and the exploitation of volatile resources.

I didn't expect the volatility of emotions and internal politics within the boardroom itself. Not to mention a startling lack of expertise—much less concern—about relevant environmental, social, and governance (ESG) sustainability issues among board members.

While that first meeting rather outdid itself in the drama department, I'd go on to see similar scenes play out in various boardrooms over the years. Since I first opened those doors, I've sat on boards on the buy side as an investor. I've also served as the founder and CEO of an asset management firm; as both a non-independent, non-executive director and an independent director; in a regulatory role; and even as chair of the board.

Over the years as both an independent and non-independent director, I've learned that trouble often arises from deeply entrenched cultural forces, intricately conflicting interests, or even brazen corruption. But perhaps more often, good decision-making gets thwarted by careless oversight and petty quarrels. In short, by human beings who, despite our fallibility, truly can—and must—do better.

CHANGING OF THE GUARD

If you've picked up this book about boardroom culture, you may be a board director—or aspiring director—yourself. Either way, you may have noticed corporate shifts toward more sustainable investing and inclusive leadership.

These trends have much to do with collaborative efforts among governments (as we'll further explore in Chapter 1). The United Nations brought together 193 world leaders in 2015 to publish 17 Sustainable Development Goals ranging from eradicating hunger to combating climate change. At the 2021 UN climate change conference in Scotland, the International Financial Reporting Standards (IFRS) launched an International Sustainability Standards Board (ISSB), now in coordination with the Global Reporting Initiative (GRI). As a result of such recent, ongoing regulatory action, board directors and executive leaders of major international corporations now routinely develop ESG sustainability reporting templates.

Yet, even as boardrooms become more ESG-focused, there's been plenty of pushback—driven by the seedier elements of what we often refer to as "politics": dishonesty, entrenched boardroom cliques, conflicts of interests, and short-sighted pursuit of the bottom line.

This is hardly news. The "old guard" has long understood that although the nature of global business patterns—and with the rise of decentralized digital currency, even the nature of money itself—changes, one thing remains constant: the power of individuals in the boardroom.

It's time we accept that while the boardroom remains a fixture in our changing world, it cannot remain fixed. It must respond, adapt, and grow. Not only to represent the interests of stockholders, but also to serve those of humanity at large and the planet we all share.

To some, this sounds lofty. Perhaps even naive.

I argue that this outlook is quite grounded and immanently realistic. Just look at how quickly our world turns upside down. As I write this, the world is still shaken by the COVID-19 pandemic, and Russia has just launched the most significant European war in eighty years. We've adapted to everything from social media to social distancing. Algorithms influence our worldviews and daily habits, and remote work has caused enormous workplace shifts. Meanwhile, climate change continues to accelerate, with urgent consequences.

If anything, I'd say it's naive to think international corporate boardrooms can go on as they have, insulating themselves against environmental and social forces, beginning and ending with the bottom line (not to mention, lining their pockets).

Besides, consumer values are shifting too, and the meteoric rise of online connectivity means greater transparency—whether corporations like it or not. Both news and rumors spread around the world almost instantly, often through images and recordings caught on cell phones. This means more whistleblowing and greater risk of exposure for corporations trying to greenwash their environmental exploitation or conceal labor abuses.

Still, the truth remains: despite promising trends, advocates for ESG sustainable investing often face fierce resistance from more established corporate board directors—at least, for now.

I believe we're about to see a substantial changing of the guard in boardrooms across the globe. As companies grasp the urgency and scope of ESG issues, they're opening seats to directors with more diverse backgrounds and perspectives than ever before—and they're looking for appointees with ESG expertise.

As of 2021, Nasdaq-listed companies must include—or publicly disclose why their board does not include—a minimum number of "diverse" directors, in terms of gender, ethnicity, and LGBTQ+ status. This move may better represent stakeholders while protecting against groupthink—though not without controversy (as we'll discuss in Chapter 2). It also creates new opportunities for corporate leaders who, like me, don't quite fit the traditional boardroom mold.

BOARDROOM POLITICS AND CULTURE

When cultures collide like this, you can expect some friction.

I should know: Southeast Asia, where I've managed money since 1988, represents the fourth largest trading partner in the world. We're a diverse group of many countries and many cultures. My asset management firm in Malaysia, Corston-Smith, has worked with partners among emerging Asian countries, as well as clients in the United States, the United Kingdom, and Canada.

As a Muslim woman raised in Malaysia by a British mother and educated in the US, I'm keenly aware that each company and country—indeed each individual board member and stakeholder—brings a unique culture to the table and helps shape boardroom politics. As these cultures and economies grow more interconnected, I believe our responsibility to each other deepens.

To both thrive personally and drive positive change, directors must not only understand what's at stake, but also deftly navigate the often ugly, real-life politics at the top. This book provides a candid, direct report from the trenches of the boardroom, based on my own firsthand experiences. While particulars have been changed or omitted to protect people and organizations (innocent or not), I've never been one to flinch from grittier elements of a situation.

In the first part of this book, I'll outline some basics every director should know about the changing politics inside the boardroom itself—with a focus on ESG issues and cross-cultural challenges ranging from diversity, equity, and inclusion (DEI) regulations to international business partnerships.

For Part 2, we'll dive deeper into ESG sustainability, outlining some of the most pressing environmental, social, and governance issues facing corporate boardrooms in the early twenty-first century.

Finally, Part 3 offers a detailed roadmap for understanding boardroom power dynamics, navigating board leadership, and better serving stakeholders through transparency, open dialogue, and, when necessary, taking an unpopular stand. This section provides practical, applied advice on how to interpret board documents, observe boardroom culture, and address red flags to become an agent for positive change.

Like many organizations, corporate boards often downplay the influence—or even existence—of internal politics. But politics certainly exists, and it drives the culture, ethics, and operations of every organization. Indeed, the political climate and internal culture within the boardroom itself can make or break a company.

ROOTED ACCOUNTABILITY, FUNDAMENTAL RESPONSIBILITY

The subtitle of this book references "radical accountability." I realize the term "radical" may induce discomfort in some readers. Indeed, it has been politicized to seem synonymous with "fanatical" or "extremist"—something inherently threatening to civilized values or social stability.

However, the earliest definition of "radical" derives from the Latin: radic-, radix, which literally means "root." From there, it came to mean "foundational" or "basic," which is the meaning I use here.

In other words, I haven't written some revolutionary call to arms to usher in a prescribed new world order of commerce. Rather, this book is a simple challenge to individuals within boardrooms to consider that our corporate decision-making can—and must—be at once profitable and *sustainable*, both socially and environmentally. That we can enrich ourselves without actively harming our communities and natural world—indeed we can and should enrich all involved.

Why? Because in the most meaningful sense, we are all stakeholders. Not only those C-level executives and investors pursuing capital returns and career advancement, but also every worker within our corporations, and every citizen of those communities we both serve and—far too frequently—disrupt.

In the mid-1990s, while representing a major investment firm, I met with a company in the region to assess a developing potential investment opportunity: a massive dam was proposed to power a hydroelectric plant for the Malaysian peninsula. When I asked how the proposed project would impact the wildlife and indigenous people dwelling in the target acreage, the CFO (who happened to be a former colleague of mine) responded with a dumbfounded look.

"Why do you care?" he asked.

Following this conversation, I was no longer invited to project updates or fund manager/analyst briefings within this company's boardroom. This was fine with me, as the initial due diligence meeting failed to meaningfully answer questions regarding process, efficacy, and even necessity of the project. Needless to say, we did not invest in the project, which would go on to displace tens of thousands of indigenous villagers and wildlife and sacrifice thousands of acres of pristine, irreplaceable rainforest to logging and flooding.

Decades later, many still refuse to take responsibility for how labor practices affect migrants, or how drilling projects impact local wildlife or communities. However, I believe we're coming to a phase in our collective history where we can no longer ignore the effects of unsustainable or harmful business practices.

Far from being some extremist, anti-business approach, recognizing that all people hold stake in the activities and consequences of global business forces us to consider the big picture and full timeline. For example: that sustainable practices—while perhaps requiring more patience and upfront costs—promise longer-term stability of profits and mutually beneficial relationships with consumers, partners, and communities.

In other words, we should care—not only because it's "the right thing to do," but also because it's just good business.

As corporate leaders in the boardroom, we can enrich ourselves while also enriching our communities and our world. To achieve both profit and sustainability, we must make better, more sustainable decisions at the highest level of international corporations—related to both internal business and related offshore entities.

Whether we lead corporations and direct investments toward making a positive difference in the world or toward destroying natural resources and harming people, our decisions impact us all in a way we can no longer sweep under the rug and ignore. We must accept that so much about how we've been doing business must—and will—change.

As board directors, I argue it's better to lead the charge toward profitable sustainability than be dragged.

The boardroom represents the highest tier of decision-making. At this level, the potential for change—both positive and negative—is profound and far-reaching. Above all, I hope my reflections empower current and future board directors—and all corporate stakeholders—to better navigate boardroom politics and help steer our interconnected cultures toward greater sustainability.

PART 1

BOARDROOM CULTURE AND POLITICS

CHAPTER 1

CHANGING WORLD, CHANGING BOARDROOM

These days, no one debates the health hazards of cigarettes. Yet, in the early 1900s, Babe Ruth's face appeared on cigarette ads, and tobacco companies sponsored every major US league baseball team. In fact, Big Tobacco sponsorship infiltrated sporting events across the globe, including—until 1984—the Olympics.

Even into the twenty-first century, tobacco companies continued to benefit from direct or indirect deals with sport organizations and athletes, such as Chinese tobacco company Baisha, which signed Olympic hurdler Liu Xiang to a promotion deal as recently as 2008. This testifies to the power of PR efforts by wealthy corporations eager to exploit consumer addiction, to the obvious detriment of public health.

We now see similar tactics exploiting our global addiction to fossil fuels. In 2020, researchers from Brown University analyzed how, for more than thirty years, some six hundred PR firms have largely shaped public discourse around climate change—for example, popularizing terms like "clean coal," "carbon footprint," and "renewable natural gas"—while shamelessly accepting payments from coal, oil and gas, steel, and utility companies.

The study amplified public criticism of the fossil fuels industry by scientists, environmental activists, and even United States lawmakers. In October 2020, a showcase congressional hearing on climate disinformation brought oil and gas executives to testify—calling to mind the 1994 Big Tobacco hearing, in which CEOs claimed innocence about the harmful effects of smoking.

Likewise, "greenwashing" efforts by PR firms have greatly influenced how we think and talk about energy, but the effects of climate change—like the health risks of tobacco—are becoming harder than ever to ignore, let alone outright deny.

As governments finally begin to grasp the reality of our heating planet, we're seeing stricter market regulations and related pressure—for example, through the votes and voices of major global pension fund shareholders—to make business more environmentally sustainable. Trends in personal and collective liability for board directors, as well as consumer values and digital connectivity, are also holding corporations more accountable for both environmental metrics and social issues like labor abuses.

I suspect it's only a matter of time before companies face a reckoning for harmful, exploitative practices related to another widespread addiction, namely our newfound dependency on cell phones, social media, and other algorithmic digital platforms, which introduce concerns about digital privacy, sociopolitical misinformation, and other exploitative practices.

In this chapter, we'll examine global trends driving the corporate shift to greater ESG sustainability, including an overview of international regulations and economic accounting standards, and how crises like the COVID-19 pandemic impact how we conduct business both on the global scale and within the boardroom.

EXPLOITATION MODEL OF BUSINESS

To succeed in business, you must check certain boxes. You need an innovative idea, first mover advantage, a large enough market, the ability to adapt, and so on. In real estate, it's location, location, location. But behind the scenes, the companies that rise most quickly to the top too often do so through exploitation.

Sure, maybe they're better-run operations with better goods and services. But look closely enough and you'll find that when a company rises considerably faster and farther than its competitors, somewhere down the supply chain, they've usually found something or someone to exploit.

Why have so many international corporations outsourced their production to China and other emerging or frontier markets in Asia and elsewhere? Because it's cheaper, of course. But how exactly do these markets maintain cheaper costs?

We all know the answer.

By employing local and migrant worker populations with limited opportunities and little to no negotiating power. Too often, opaque and unenforced local labor laws (especially for migrant workers) in such markets involve abusive hiring agencies, unjust contracts, poverty wages, and dismal worker conditions—while turning a blind eye to forced labor and worse. This international outsourcing also serves to hollow out manufacturing industries in certain countries while building it up in other, cheaper (for the moment) locations.

Meanwhile, the exploitation of fossil fuels has undoubtedly revolutionized the way we live and interact with one another around the world. However, for all the progress we've gained through the industrial and now digital revolutions, we're now faced with potentially existential risks from that same progress: mounting plastic pollution, rising global temperatures, extreme weather events like massive floods and droughts, wildfires, and rising sea levels.

EXPLOITATION IN THE DIGITAL AGE

On one hand, it's easy to see how digital progress—the ubiquity of cell phones and the internet—has educated us, reducing ignorance about and therefore also tolerance of this traditional exploitation model. In many ways, corporate abuses were more overt decades ago. Back in the 1990s, consumers may have heard reports of sweatshops in Asia associated with major US companies, but the news traveled slowly and spottily, making it much easier for consumers to miss or ignore—and for companies to hide from investors in their supply chain.

Consumers are now far more connected and savvy, thanks to near-universal access to pocket-sized computers/cameras/audio and video recorders through which anyone can instantly share reports, images, and videos with friends and strangers around the world. The ability for any citizen—or worker, or individual within a boardroom for that matter—to surreptitiously snap a photo or video and blast across the globe presents brand new liabilities for companies still eager to exploit. This has completely and permanently heightened the risk of exposure for corporations behaving badly.

That said, this same hyperconnectivity is lousy with deeply entrenched—and often shameless—social exploitation of its own. Just look at the controversies surrounding Mark Zuckerberg's Meta platforms. Whistleblowers such as former Facebook product manager Frances Haugen claim the company has knowingly amplified hate, misinformation, and political divisions. Such content disproportionately impacts vulnerable populations, including children impressionable to distortions of self-image or dangerous worldviews. Meanwhile, these platforms raise serious questions about both data protection and risks associated with undeclared or unenforceable user age restriction.

With its advertising revenue linked to user views and clicks, social media operates according to a classic economy of scale—rife for exploitation. Unfortunately, it's hard to deny that strong emotions like fear and hate really do sell. Meanwhile, finding some way to, for example, actually enforce age limits on these sites would cut into their user base and therefore also their profit margins.

But is this approach sustainable? Is it worth the social costs—not to mention the risk of current and future backlash from the young people injured by these practices (and their loved ones)? Is there really no other way to profit than through excessive and willful destruction?

I believe that, as both innovative corporate leaders and human beings, we can be smarter than that.

SHAREHOLDER PRESSURE

Despite decades of unaccountable corporate exploitation, there are reasons to be optimistic. More companies are setting and maintaining ESG sustainability standards, in part because shareholders increasingly expect it—and they're pushing their investments and retirement funds (such as pensions, mutual funds, managed funds, hedge funds) to expect it.

Institutional investors come in many different forms—representing different organizational and governance structures and subject to different regulatory requirements. This ecosystem ranges from mutual funds and ETFs (regulated in the US by the Security and Exchange Commission) to pension funds, insurance companies, and a wide variety of (relatively unregulated) hedge funds and managed accounts.

The role and influence of institutional investors in capital markets has exploded since the mid-twentieth century, in part due to a dramatic increase in overall market capitalization. In 1950, the combined market value of all stocks listed on the New York Stock Exchange (NYSE) was about $94 billion. By 2012, however, the domestic market capitalization of the NYSE was more than $14 trillion—an increase of nearly 1,500 percent. This growth is even more impressive if you add the $4.5 trillion in market capitalization on the Nasdaq market, which, until 1971, did not exist. The bottom line is that, as a whole, institutional investors own a much larger share of a larger market.

Recent changes in market structure and trading technologies have contributed to this growth in institutionally managed assets. These include the development of the US national market system, the proliferation of trading venues—such as dark pools and electronic trading platforms—and the advent of algorithmic and high-speed trading. These changes, largely driven by institutional investor trading, have resulted in huge increases in trading volumes.

Clearly, institutional investors enjoy enormous, growing power in our capital markets. And, as Franklin Delano Roosevelt put it, in his 1945 address to the American people, "great power involves great responsibility."

For institutional investors, the central responsibility lies in their stewardship of assets belonging to others—namely, millions of workers, policyholders, retirees, and other individual investors. These people entrust their monies to institutional investors to help them save, increase their disposable income, and provide a safe and secure retirement.

Just as tobacco-free retirement funds gained popularity, policyholders have started looking to higher standards when it comes to environmental and social sustainability. State public employee and teacher pension funds across the US, as well as companies such as CalSTRS, TIAA-CREF, BlackRock, Vanguard, and the British Telecom Pension Scheme (BTPS) all reflect this change, as do UN PRI signatories around the world—especially in Europe, Canada, and Australia, and increasingly across Asia as well.

Norway's Government Pension Fund Global—which grew to the largest sovereign wealth fund in the world thanks to North Sea oil supplies—recently got global attention for divesting from oil and gas companies. Instead, they now aim to convert wealth originally amassed through exploitation of fossil fuels into ESG sustainable investments around the world.

This move demonstrates that, while exploitation is a choice, so is accountability. The old uber-competitive, opportunistic methods may bring handsome short-term gains, but the reality is they've become too risky—not only for natural resources and exploited communities, but also for our companies themselves.

The growing emphasis on environmental and social impact and corporate sustainability has increased shareholder pressure on companies. The message is: If you want this capital, operate more responsibly. How can you manage your business to help ensure our Earth doesn't heat beyond 1.5 degrees Celsius? How are you avoiding or addressing labor abuses and community complaints about such matters as job creation or pollution and waste? How are you encouraging a broader representation of people and perspectives within your boardroom?

As we'll explore next, broad and largely undefined international government regulations are also moving toward more precise—if not yet strictly enforceable—ESG standards and recommendations. Meanwhile, major developments regarding international board liability have upped the ante when it comes to holding global businesses accountable.

UN PRINCIPLES FOR RESPONSIBLE INVESTMENT

Back in 2005, the United Nations, then led by Secretary General Kofi Annan, hosted a group of major institutional investors from around the world to develop the Principles for Responsible Investment (PRIs).

They put together six PRIs and invited companies to become signatories, affirming a commitment to incorporating ESG sustainability into investment analyses, policies, and practices. (BTPS was founding Chair.) Among other things, signatories agree to both seek ESG disclosure from entities they invest in and report on their own activities and progress.

From 2005 until 2008—when asset management firm Corston-Smith signed on—there were very few PRI signatories. However, as of 2022, we number around 3,800 signatories, impacting trillions of dollars of managed assets.

Still, at the time of this book's publication, I feel PRI could do more to engage its signatories, help lead the discussion, and deepen everyone's commitment. On the surface, they're doing something virtuous. However, many companies feel frustrated by onerous PRI reporting standards, and the fact that they're charged a percentage of assets to become signatories. Meanwhile, there's a lack of meaningful enforcement of PRI principles, leading many companies to disingenuously hop on the PRI bandwagon just to check a box and avoid industry blacklisting.

UN SUSTAINABLE DEVELOPMENT GOALS

In 2015, a decade after the United Nations launched its PRIs, it held a general assembly to develop seventeen interconnected sustainable development goals as a "blueprint to achieve a better and more sustainable future for all" by 2030. Unlike the UN Millennium Development Goals preceding them (in 2000), SDGs apply to all nations, not just those considered "developing" or "emerging." Indeed, 193 countries signed onto SDGs in 2015.

The SDGs range in scope from reducing inequalities to eliminating hunger to promoting responsible consumption and production. Together, these goals form a broad and noble vision of ESG sustainability—and they certainly energized global dialogue on ESG, prompting those countries represented to take fuller account of national and global sustainability issues. However, SDGs remain too vague, broad, and nonbinding. It's not like the UN can sack you for operating in or with a country that hasn't meaningfully enforced SDG #6, for example.

That said, some major stock exchanges have begun revising listing requirements to encourage annual ESG sustainability reports for shareholders. Few *binding* listing rules or mandates related to ESG have emerged, but stock exchange pressure has prompted many companies to set up sustainability committees and include ESG updated templates in their reports. These updated templates explain measures to reduce diesel emissions or reuse plastics, disclose supply chain declarations, and develop supply codes of ethics.

At the end of the day, SDGs are there for both government and corporate leaders to use as a guide, to set priorities and establish leadership in this shifting tide of ESG sustainability. And in my experience, such guidance is sorely needed. Many international boards still lack expertise in sustainable investing principles (at home and abroad). Meanwhile, from independent directors serving publicly listed companies to trustees representing asset owners, those pushing for positive change fight the inertia of decades of exploitative business practices.

ACCOUNTING STANDARDS

While ESG guiding principles and priorities are nice things to have, what the world needs now is true transparency and accountability—which is to say, something standardized, measurable, and enforceable.

That's just what the International Financial Reporting Standards (IFRS) Foundation aimed to do at the 2021 UN Climate Change Conference COP26 when they set up an International Sustainability Standards Board (ISSB) to draft accounting standards for ESG.

The IFRS have been adopted by more than 144 countries, with the notable exception of the US, whose Securities and Exchange Commission (SEC) instead uses its own set of rule-based standards called the Generally Accepted Accounting Principles (GAAP). While the SEC has suggested it intends to move toward adopting IFRS, progress has stalled on that front, complicating efforts to create one set of clear, enforceable accounting standards around the globe.

In the past, accounting standards like the IFRS and GAAP (pronounced "gap") have done much to reduce corporate financial misconduct and improve governance standards. For example, directors of multiple publicly listed companies used to be able to raise money earmarked for one company and instead give it to a related sister company with no legal or even negative consequences.

Now, this sort of thing rarely happens, because it's a clear breach. The international adoption of transparent and enforceable accounting standards has also made it harder (but not impossible) for corrupt individuals and groups to launder money and offer or accept bribes—which until the late twentieth century was not even recognized by many governments as a crime.

In short, measures such as the IFRS and the US Foreign Corrupt Practices Act (FCPA) have already transformed global business simply by holding companies to formal standards against dodgy practices and ill-gotten gains—and they're beginning to do the same for ESG. But while these moves are promising, their adoption will take years and may remain limited. Particularly when it comes to incorporating a legally binding, enforceable ESG metric.

That's where IFRS and GAAP hold an advantage: their accounting principles can be enforced by the US SEC and equivalent regulatory authorities worldwide. Indeed, the US SEC will soon require publicly listed companies to publicly disclose their environmental impact according to set standards and metrics. Even better, they've begun enacting fines on asset management firms who falsely claim to promote ESG products and practices, which should do much to reduce greenwashing and outright investor fraud.

After all, companies rarely adjust their behavior unless they get hit in the purse.

US SEC DISCLOSURE RULES

In June 2022, the US SEC published new proposed disclosure rules for funds and advisers claiming to integrate ESG sustainability measures into their investment products and services. These rules set disclosure standards for investors and reduce the risk of greenwashing through exaggerated or misrepresented ESG claims.

Such proposals reflect growing investor interest in ESG issues— and the resulting proliferation of investment products and services marketed as "green" or "sustainable" without clear criteria related to ESG-related attributes or methodologies. The SEC's proposed new rules identify investment products with various levels of ESG centrality to their strategies, requiring different disclosures for environmental, social, and governance standards, respectively.

For example, in 2022, the US SEC fined BNY Mellon Investment Adviser $1.5 million for "misstatements and omissions" related to its ESG investment policies for some of its managed mutual funds. And they're not the only organization under scrutiny. Also in 2022, the US SEC sued the publicly traded Brazilian mining company Vale for allegedly making false and misleading disclosures about the safety of its dams ahead of a 2019 disaster that killed 270 people. Vale faced charges of manipulating dam safety audits, obtaining fraudulent stability certificates, and misleading governments, communities, and investors with its ESG disclosures.

Unfortunately, regulators in many emerging markets hesitate to adopt or enforce standards such as those adopted by the US SEC. In some countries, publicly listed companies and other regulated entities violating environmental, social, or governance standards are beholden only to the regulating authority that enforces such breaches. This potentially allows company directors to cozy up to regulators.

As we'll discuss next, China and other more developed markets in Asia have also developed platforms for investors to take on errant directors and companies. However, certain smaller markets in Southeast Asia lag behind. Within these latter regions, cultural norms and patterns are more permissive toward ESG abuses, and the smaller investor has no ad hoc legal aid available. Meanwhile, powerful companies and directors in breach of ESG standards appear to enjoy blind protection by authorities.

LIABILITY

In 2021, the world saw China's first class action lawsuit against corporate fraud. In this landmark case, a pharmaceutical company manipulated the numbers by USD$4.8 billion between 2016 and 2018. Chinese shareholders got so angry that fifty-five thousand of them came together and sued.

Before this case, the maximum amount a Chinese board director could get fined was about 94,000 US dollars. In 2021, the Chinese government changed that to a percentage of ill-gotten gains. Suddenly these directors, pulling in annual board fees of only around $31,000, could be fined $19 million.

No longer can such directors get away with saying they're innocent of charges because they failed to understand management's papers to the board or didn't fully read the captured board meeting minutes. Suddenly, board members can be held directly responsible for the public impact of underhanded boardroom dealings.

The result? Panic and retreat, evidenced by mass resignations of board directors in about twenty different Asian companies.

The United States also allows class suits against company boards. As I write this, one such suit is underway against a company from Singapore that has listed in New York. A group of investors recently lost great sums of money even as the company founders paid themselves fat sums. A half a dozen law firms have jumped on the suit.

Meaningful ESG standards, liability, and other financial consequences for company leaders may indeed complicate the lives of board members, holding them to higher standards—and at higher risk. However, considering the stakes of global environmental and social issues, I believe board members inclined toward foundational accountability can and should welcome these trends overall.

COVID-19

In the height of the COVID-19 pandemic, boardroom tensions ran very high. "Business as usual" dissolved and everyone flew into survival mode. In boardrooms around the world, some directors became increasingly aggressive, banging tables, lobbying like mad to keep commerce open for their specific vested interests.

In Southeast Asia, the first blow hit our tourism industry and its interconnected ecosystem of travel, hospitality, and entertainment. Meanwhile, many poor migrant laborers went into hiding, scared of deportation or infection. Not only were medical-related industries everywhere overwhelmed and underprepared, but also economic safety nets largely failed to support people and corporations through global lockdowns.

Corporations around the world moved urgently to protect the safety of workers and consumers. Retailers offered new delivery services. Companies allowed office staff to work remotely, adopting new IT products and boosting digital security. Consumers adapted to new forms of digital communication and remote operations, and businesses and individuals alike discovered new opportunities to directly exchange goods, services, and cash through nascent digital services.

Long before recent events such as the COVID-19 pandemic and Russian invasion of Ukraine, I'd worked through several global and regional geopolitical crises—from the 1987 Black Monday Crash and the 1997–98 Asian Financial Crisis to the 2000 dot com bubble, 9/11, the Global Financial Crisis of 2007–09, and the European Sovereign Debt Crisis of 2011. I can attest that such events make good corporate leaders more savvy, responsive, and adaptable.

There's a saying in my part of the world that "when New York sneezes, we all catch pneumonia." Indeed, within every global and regional crisis I've witnessed, I've seen some degree of financial contagion. For example, the 1997–98 Asian Financial Crisis began with mismanaged foreign debt in Bangkok that unpegged the Thai baht from the US dollar. This soon set off a cascade of currency devaluation in multiple countries across Southeast Asia.

As I write this, many markets affected by the Asian Financial Crisis still have not recovered their pre-1997 value.

Still, such crises necessarily test and refine financial markets, resulting in improvised new contingency plans, communications infrastructure, and business continuity processes—at least, among healthy corporations.

What happens if there's a new war, a massive flood, another pandemic? If email goes down, how do you reach people? Is your data safe from security breaches while employees work from home?

How do you properly conduct general meetings with shareholders over a remote video platform?

At the highest level of corporate decision-making, the truly global scale of COVID-19 served as both a wakeup call and a harbinger of things to come in our age of unprecedented global interconnectedness. Corporations that survive the destabilizing effects of pandemics, climate disasters, and other global crises will be those that think outside of the box—and those that privilege big-picture and long-term sustainability over more vulnerable short-term gains.

Global upheavals like COVID-19 show us not only the vulnerability of our interdependence, but also how quickly and profoundly we can collaborate, adapt, and transform. I believe that, moving forward, ESG sustainability will be considered mandatory knowledge for successful boards. The COVID-19 pandemic and other recent global phenomena have served to accelerate the shift toward sustainability and radical accountability, inspiring more focused metrics when it comes to ESG regulations.

We're connected by so much more than goods and services. We dramatically impact one another's public health and well-being. Indeed, one hopeful effect of this devastating global health crisis seems to be a realization among corporate and government leaders that sustainability is more than "good PR." Indeed, it's the only way forward.

Stakeholder awareness of corporations' impact on society and the environment is changing at the grassroots level as consumers, employees, and local communities become more vocal about their concerns. Consumer consciousness around these issues—from packaging and single-use plastics, to concerns about the carbon footprint of meat production, to labor conditions in apparel manufacturing—affects a wide range of industries.

Meanwhile, public perception has become more prevalent through the use of social media and other communication platforms. This all intensified as companies navigated the immediate, worldwide social impact of COVID-19. The devastating pandemic influenced public attitudes toward sustainability, leading to considerable growth in ESG sustainable funds and incentives for green finance instruments.

Boardroom liability is also changing rapidly, as both consumers and shareholders demand more transparency and ethical conduct. Meanwhile, corporations must adapt to and prepare for the possibility of more global crises moving forward.

As we'll explore in the next chapters, boards are beginning to appreciate the benefits of ESG sustainability—and they're beginning to look for directors with expertise in environmental, social, and governance sustainability. In some parts of the world, they're also incentivized to expand the diversity of their corporate leadership, largely in response to cultural changes, consumer pressure, and corporate moves like DEI listing requirements on stock exchanges like Nasdaq and the London Stock Exchange.

CHAPTER 2

DEI AND GROUPTHINK

Years after I walked through the doors of a boardroom for the first time, I convened my first meeting as a board chair. In both instances (and many others in between), I was the first multiracial (English and Malaysian) woman to serve in the role.

By the time of the latter experience, I was so accustomed to my nontraditional status that I wasn't thinking much about it—until something odd happened. Something I'd never seen happen to a newly minted chairman (emphasis on the "man").

No sooner had I begun to address the assembled directors and company executives than a senior independent director stood up. Out of the corner of my eye, I saw him cross over to a large automatic espresso machine and start making himself a coffee—while I was mid-sentence.

Maybe it was the acoustics of the room, but I'd never before appreciated the cacophony of grinding and frothing these machines produce alongside cappuccinos and lattes. It sounded like a miniature power drill had struck a tiny bubbling hot spring.

Not inclined to shout, I paused. The entire—quite large—roomful of senior management teams and I patiently waited for the noise to subside so I could recommence the meeting.

Within minutes, another director stood, walked to the table, and made himself a coffee. Once again, we all waited out the clamor before I continued.

Finally, a third person—the CEO himself—got up and crossed to the table. This time, upon interrupting the meeting, the man casually chatted to me from the coffee table as though we were lounging in a Starbucks.

While I appreciate the value of caffeinated drinks in executive decision-making, this seemed a clear—and rather cartoonish—power play, a childish prank by powerful men to literally drown out the voice of someone who didn't match the conventional profile of a leader.

Ridiculously enough, it called to mind a scene in *Austin Powers*: every time Dr. Evil attempts to explain his master plan to the cabinet, Bad Guy Number Two cranks on a similarly deafening espresso machine. At that moment, I understood why the chief villain responded with such colorful threats.

Instead I said, "Would somebody please remove that coffee machine? Take it out to the lounge. If anyone would like to make coffee, please go outside."

Although this was my moment to set a new tone of leadership, some of these men seemed intent on setting a tone of their own. I've spoken to other executives who—due to gender, ethnicity, or sexual orientation—challenge conventional notions of corporate leadership within their cultural context. Each individual has stories reflecting some level of perceived discriminatory pushback. Sometimes, this behavior is just subtle or innocuous enough for plausible deniability. And I believe that—like any childish bullying—it's designed to test limits and expose weakness, through either tolerance of disrespect or a disproportionate, emotional response.

I reminded myself that, generally speaking, men have a history of testing—indeed sometimes fiercely hazing—other men in power as well, even those sharing their cultural and sociopolitical backgrounds. And there I was, a half-British woman overseeing top-level financial decisions within a powerful Southeast Asian corporate entity.

During times like these, I'm reminded of the fortitude of my maternal lineage. In 1916, before women in the United Kingdom could vote, Mathilda Daisy Palmer—my grandmother—graduated from the University of London with a bachelor of arts in Latin, mechanics, and geography, while simultaneously earning her teaching qualifications.

My mother, Dr. Gwendolen Daisy Smith, was a greatly influential pediatric physician, and intensely principled woman, who met my father after he came to the UK to study law at London's Middle Temple. She moved with my father first to Singapore and then current-day Malaysia after World War II. After leaving everything she knew and traveling across an ocean, she went on to co-found a private hospital that has since become one of the largest healthcare organizations in the region.

Given this family history of courageous, pioneering women and men, I knew how those parts of me that didn't quite fit the mold in Southeast Asia had actually supported my leadership journey—and I knew the perspective and value they brought to the situation at hand. At the very least, I certainly knew how to "keep calm and carry on."

GROUPTHINK

In the late 1990s, when Volvo was designing their XC90 sport utility vehicle, they assembled an advisory panel of twenty-four California women. That model sold so well that Volvo sent out a self-congratulatory press release lauding its decision to listen to women, thereby providing representatives of their majority buyer group the "pride of authorship that comes from being a major influence in the development of a vehicle."

Taken one step further, by privileging female representation within its own boardroom, a company could benefit from representing this full *half of humanity* as a matter of course. But of course, it would take a bit more time for this revolutionary concept to catch on.

As I write this, DEI are popular corporate letters, which significantly overlap with the starring acronym of this book: ESG. Most notably, the "S" portion. While some prefer to dismiss matters of diversity, equity, and inclusion as banners of politically correct "virtue signaling" or social justice wars, in the business world return on investment is key. As we'll explore in a moment, various studies indicate that companies with more diverse boards enjoy greater financial gains.

Why? I believe much of it comes down to avoiding groupthink.

Imagine that your company's senior management and independent directors all hail from the same cultural and socioeconomic backgrounds. They think and behave similarly, attended the same schools, and moved through similar professional trajectories. (Not very hard to imagine, is it?)

Now, unless the overwhelming majority of your consumer base also shares the exact cultural, socioeconomic, and educational influences as your board members—not to mention their same patterns of thinking and behavior—your board will not consistently and accurately provide the best value for your target consumer market.

As a result, your board will often allocate resources and investments into the wrong ideas and end up spending a fortune on outside consultants and focus groups. You risk devolving into an echo chamber of groupthink and yes-people disconnected from the reality of your customer base. Whether true or not, there's a reason why some have quipped that if the Lehman Brothers had been the Lehman Sisters, they wouldn't have collapsed.

The idea is that more diverse, inclusive leadership can help challenge assumptions, provide new perspectives, represent broader swaths of the public, and protect against blind spots. Indeed, multiple studies have shown that companies with women directors demonstrate more stable financial performance metrics—including research conducted by my own asset management group, Corston-Smith, in Malaysia in 2011.

For our ASEAN 5 Gender Diversity, Equity, and Inclusion project, we analyzed 3,054 companies in Southeast Asia and Hong Kong in terms of six objective financial variables to see how the performance of those companies with women directors compared to the performance against the market valuations. We could conclusively see that companies with at least one woman on the board outperformed on all financial benchmarks, including revenue, market capitalization, net profit, return on equity, return on assets, and earnings per share. Those companies with up to three women directors did even better.

One question is whether it was the women directors themselves that added the deciding value. Alternatively, perhaps the more diverse companies already had innovative leaders who valued different perspectives and therefore naturally avoided groupthink—hence their interest in appointing women to the board.

Either way, these research findings on financial performance indicators helped inspire the Malaysian government to propose a one-third target, encouraging major companies to aim for at least 30 percent representation of women within boardrooms. This proposal received cabinet approval back in 2011.

However, in 2022, we at Corston-Smith conducted another research project on Bursa Malaysia (Malaysian Stock Exchange), finding that of the top 100 Malaysian companies, 58 did not meet the 30 percent target for women board directors—mainly because this target was just a recommendation rather than a formal mandate.

So what happens when such DEI targets are meaningfully enforced? Interestingly, in 2022 the Malaysian government finally did formally mandate "at least one woman on all publicly listed boards." While some hail this official mandate as social progress, it actually represents a step backward from the previously stated (though unenforceable) goal of women accounting for 30 percent of publicly listed board directors.

As we'll discuss next, this more modest government mandate likely comes in response to similar DEI-related listing requirements in the US and Britain.

NASDAQ DEI LISTING REQUIREMENTS

In 2020, the US SEC approved a proposal requiring all Nasdaq-listed companies to have, or publicly explain why they don't have, at least two "diverse" directors, including at least one who self-identifies as a woman and at least one who self-identifies as an underrepresented minority or LGBTQ+.

The following year, Britain's financial regulator, the Financial Conduct Authority, proposed similar requirements for their nation's largest firms, and other stock exchanges are likely to follow suit (or pantsuit, as the case may be).

The move to represent more diverse populations on boards—despite the snail's pace of such efforts in the first two decades of the twenty-first century—is part of a larger point of groupthink-related debate among corporate directors over "board composition refresh."

For the most part, directors tend to grow accustomed to their seats. Many companies keep even their so-called *independent* directors, with neither will nor incentive to step down, for ten to twelve years or more—sometimes for the entire lifespan of a business. Unless companies expand their boards, I find it unlikely that DEI requirements will be achieved in the near future. Compounding issues of access and opportunity is the fact that once a director gains a board seat, they often go on to join multiple other corporate boards—and this is true of both men and women.

Granted, institutional knowledge and experience are vital strengths. Also, both nimble thinking and market savvy are possible at any age. But at some point, it becomes difficult to avoid groupthink or keep up with rapidly changing issues without some new blood. Shifting social attitudes and company culture—accelerated by corporate responses in 2020 to the George Floyd protests and Black Lives Matter movement—have brought a new layer to the debate over board composition refresh.

To some extent, the Nasdaq listing requirements trickle down from the UN Sustainable Development Goals (SDG #6)—and they're creating a cottage industry of training programs, many of which claim to prepare women for board director positions. On one hand, it's exciting to see the promise of unprecedented opportunities open up for women and other groups historically underrepresented in the corporate boardroom. On the other hand, sudden cultural shifts tend to spark friction as established power structures adapt—or resist.

RESISTANCE AND ADAPTATION

As I've experienced firsthand, cultural patterns can run deep, and those accustomed to unchecked power don't appreciate the mandate to share it—especially when newcomers dare to challenge entrenched views, values, and unconscious biases.

I understand the logic and intention behind the DEI listing requirements in such developed markets as the US and UK markets, because I believe increased diversity and inclusion in both domestic and international boardrooms will positively impact how we conduct global business—both in terms of ESG sustainability and in terms of the corporate financial metrics that shape overall market stability.

That said, as the demographics of corporate decision-makers shift, we must brace ourselves for increased political disruption in the boardroom.

Board directors who don't fit the mold can safely expect some challenges, ranging from subtle power plays and attempts to discredit to criticisms based on appearance, as well as practical inconveniences—for example, the location and relative cleanliness of the women's restroom, or lack of nonbinary restroom facilities.

SYMBOLISM, RELIGION, AND CULTURAL NORMS

Often, tensions arise more from cultural symbolism than actual business matters. I once attended an event with no formally communicated dress code. When I arrived, I was the only board member dressed in a suit; everyone else wore traditional cultural costumes. This is akin to not wearing the corporate T-shirt to a company outing when literally every other member of the board and executive team somehow got the (unofficial) memo.

From Western business attire and company shirts to saris and Baju Kurungs, our dress codes reflect more than mere fashion statements; they are also symbols that can be weaponized. Meanwhile, deviations from culturally accepted attire may be valid choices prompting much-needed dialogue and cultural adjustment—but not without first creating some waves. Imagine, for example, a cisgendered man donning a dress to a board meeting of directors long accustomed to conservative suits and ties. A symbolic gesture such as this would provoke because it challenges notions of gender identity and tradition.

In short, worldviews often clash dramatically. What one culture may consider an inalienable right, another may deem a punishable crime, particularly when informed by religious doctrine. Some traditional religions, for example, maintain moral misgiving about divorce and remarriage, but in secular societies, these religious views now have limited influence over official family law.

Yet even in the secular West, older generations tend to exhibit less tolerance for the LGBTQ+ community, based on cultural norms largely rooted in matters of faith and morality. I remember former US president Barack Obama admitting that listening to his children informed his evolving views on same-sex marriage as a civil right. Meanwhile, in many parts of Asia and the Middle East, same-sex intimate relations—let alone marriage—remain strictly prohibited by (cultural acceptance and/or) law. As a result, Western board members visiting these countries should not be surprised if they and their same-sex spouse fail to receive event invitations.

Religious norms aside, sometimes the cultural dissonance is downright petty. I recall one international business event hosted in New York earlier in my career. There, a junior Asian fund manager—a woman of petite build—quietly endured jokes by her supervisor regarding her body. In some cultures, tolerance for such crude personal critiques of the female body continues—even in professional contexts. When New York directors caught wind of the conversation, they immediately walked away (decades before cultural movements like #metoo reshaped the dialogue on—and consequences of—gender-based harassment and assault).

I bring this up not to gossip or gripe, but to point out that, in my experience, boardroom politics can get messy, trifling, and even downright vulgar. As cultural norms shift toward greater diversity, equity, and inclusion, new opportunities will crop up. That's both encouraging and vitally important for social sustainability in global business. However, it's important that women and traditionally underrepresented groups prepare themselves for the range of discordant cultural and political values at play on the other side of the boardroom doors.

DISCREDITING, GROOMING, AND MORE

Early in my fund management career, colleagues referred to me as the "managing director's recruit"—MDR for short—because the managing director personally knew my mother.

Now, to call my mother principled would be a laughable understatement. This woman followed my father from her native London to Southeast Asia. There she co-founded a specialist hospital, where she worked until the age of seventy-five, treating over a million people. She not infrequently kept VIPs waiting as she attended to pediatric patients. I'm told that in the 1960s, she once halted mid-speech to inform a pregnant audience member about the dangers of smoking—and she calmly refused to continue her talk until the woman extinguished her cigarette.

In 2014, when Forbes listed me among "Asia's 50 Power Business-women," my mother asked in a tone of genuine skepticism what I'd done to warrant such acknowledgment. In short, she'd never have dreamed of intervening to advance my career.

Reflecting back, plenty of men around me *had* made their way into powerful positions through direct or indirect influence of relatives, friends, and associates—and *unabashedly* so. They called this "shrewd networking." But when it's a woman or minority, suddenly everything takes on a different tone.

This is not to say that nepotism never extends to women and underrepresented groups, as well. I've seen companies padding their "DEI numbers" with the daughters or wives of previous—or even current—independent directors. At one such company, a woman executive referred to these individuals as "inherited independent of directors." Of course, this sort of thing occurs with directors' sons as well, and in both situations the practice indeed compromises the meaning of the term "independent."

Still, I've found that when a woman ascends within a male-dominated sphere, she's far more often met with greater suspicion and less reliable support—sometimes outright smears. Throughout my career, I've come to accept that not everyone who appears to be an ally actually wants me to succeed. Indeed, at times I've felt set up as pure collateral damage.

This sort of treatment can apply to other underrepresented groups as well, and it can impel "diverse directors" to keep quiet and defer to conventional views and practices. Sometimes this is due to informal grooming that results from increased scrutiny; other times it's because all board appointees—regardless of gender, background, and sexual identity—are selected based on how well they already agree with current leadership or conform to those leaders' views on how, for example, a woman should behave. When this happens, "diversity" alone will not prevent groupthink.

I've sat on boards where my fellow women directors remain mute throughout meetings, then conspicuously prattle on about baking recipes and housekeeping hacks after meetings adjourn. While I'm happy to share culinary tips in the right time and place, say while hosting a dinner party, there tend to be more pressing matters to discuss surrounding board meetings.

Behavior of this sort risks communicating to other women that their input should be limited to socially acceptable spheres. It's particularly concerning given that outside of board meetings, vital off-record conversations occur. Yes, small talk abounds— often surrounding the more male-accepted topic of professional sports. While it may represent an unfair double standard, I have seen domestic chatter cut women off from vital, unofficial news flow.

MENTORS AND SPONSORS

Representation at the top level of a company means so much for younger professionals. When a junior woman, person of color, or LGBTQ+ individual sees someone who looks like or identifies similarly to them making executive decisions, they realize there's potential for their own upward mobility. This can inspire employees to engage deeper with and invest more into their work.

Everyone benefits from both early and ongoing professional role models and active support. This helps explain the volume of programs claiming to mentor women and minorities and help them achieve board positions. However, I know a number of women who've invested in such courses only to report weak returns.

In my opinion, there's no substitute for active support from colleagues within an organization. When advocating for junior staff, I find that women *mentor*, while men *sponsor*. Women may advise younger female employees about corporate politics and practices over lunch, or provide unofficial feedback. Meanwhile, men seem more likely to actively endorse their younger male cohorts and recommend their advancement. It's my view that, to move up the corporate ladder, women and underrepresented groups need not only models of success and friendly mentors, but proactive *sponsors* advocating for them as well.

CARVING OUT—AND DEFENDING—YOUR SPACE

While the noisy male espresso parade during my first meeting as board chair was particularly disruptive, I sensed quieter gestures of disrespect at play. As I directed that meeting, I noticed how unusually close the men on either side of me sat, and how they'd lean yet closer to glance down at my notes—indirect boundary pushing I'd never before experienced, nor witnessed toward a male board chair.

In addition to transferring the espresso machine out of the room, I had the board secretary remove the two chairs next to mine in advance of subsequent meetings.

Such experiences often lead very senior women and minorities to likewise maintain strict protocols for their space. I was speaking once at a high-profile general meeting in Japan where all speakers were given a car. When one man's car failed to show up, he asked a female political leader to share hers. Through her aide, she declined to offer him a ride. Based on the salty gossip I later overheard, he complained through the grapevine, and to many directors, this woman appeared irrationally fussy.

Given my personal experiences, I understood perfectly. When you've had a long day of meetings, the last thing you want is somebody to observe how tired you are and report on it to others. Heaven forbid you should let yourself doze off in the presence of someone who might feel entitled to snap a photo and share it in jest on social media. Whether a matter of safety or respect, it's important to carve out and defend your space.

Returning to the espresso incident, I've heard a curious number of stories from women regarding men and coffee. In the early 2000s, I spoke at an event headlined by then US Secretary of State Condoleezza Rice and Dame Jenny Shipley. Ms. Rice related to me and others the time she was first invited to a Pentagon meeting. She walked in—the only woman and the only Black person in the room—and one of the generals turned to her and said something like, "The rookie makes the coffee."

Rice recalled asking herself, "Is this really the standard tradition, or something else? Should I politely decline or be a good sport?" In the end, she prepared and served coffee for that roomful of men. But she confessed she just might have added disproportionate amounts of sugar to the pot to subtly express her objection to (and ensure subsequent exemption from) coffee duty. In short, she played along—but not without getting in a subtle jab of her own.

This response demonstrates the combination of grace and fortitude often needed when navigating boardroom politics—particularly when you don't fit the mold of conventional leadership.

Having examined recent trends toward greater ESG accountability and shifting boardroom demographics, let's close Part 1 with some practical takeaways. The next chapter will more closely examine what any ESG-minded board newcomer can expect, and how all directors and stakeholders can maneuver boardroom culture and politics in the service of greater sustainability.

CHAPTER 3

WANT TO DO GOOD?
BRING THE GOODS

Back in the early 1990s, just a few years into my career as a fund manager, I spoke in the ballroom of the Waldorf Astoria resort in downtown Manhattan before a rather large assembly to promote AIG Investment Corporation's Southeast Asia fund. During my talk, a man in the audience raised his hand. I invited him to speak, and he asked, "Are you really Muslim?"

When I said "yes," he remarked, "Well, you look and sound very different."

To that, I laughed and said, "I think I am different. I have an English mother."

Decades later, comments like his would be considered impolite at best. At the time though, there was no cultural sensitivity training, no DEI initiatives. Most Americans had little to no contact with ordinary Muslims, and their ideas of my culture were largely informed by popular entertainment, alarming current events like the Iran hostage situation in the early 1980s, and (often sensational) political rhetoric. I could sense this man was sincerely intrigued.

My response seemed to break the ice, suggesting that he was not the only person confused by this Muslim woman dressed in a suit addressing a professional crowd in a semi-British accent.

The way I saw it, I was a guest in the USA, representing an international branch of a US company. I was there to share knowledge; I wanted them to know that Southeast Asia is an exciting part of the world. I understood that people may say insensitive things—more often motivated by innocent curiosity than by malice. Throughout my career, whether speaking in a crowded ballroom, chairing the AGM of a board, or even chatting informally with shareholders, I've found it's always best not to take such things personally.

This is especially important as Nasdaq listing requirements and other developing DEI regulations around the globe incentivize greater representation. This will feel to some like coercive, politically correct "affirmative action," inspiring everything from unconscious resentment to deliberate pushback.

Perhaps you are a director or aspiring director from an underrepresented demographic. Or maybe you hail from a more conventional background, *and* you also value ESG sustainability and support diversity, equity, and inclusion in the boardroom. Either way, I and others are proof that you can succeed in the boardroom while advocating ESG sustainable business practices.

I'm not going to lie and say that discrimination—whether related to race, religion, gender, or sexual orientation—no longer exists, or that you can avoid it with the right attitude. I do, however, advise against letting discrimination become the defining narrative of your career.

Meanwhile, the fact remains that many people—at every echelon of society or sphere of influence—make decisions based on pure emotion, self-interest, or unsound motives. It's one thing when the stakes are low, but on a public board of directors, you're truly standing at the pinnacle of an organization. What you think and say and do can make a huge impact.

Every new director impacts and alters boardroom culture, and therefore company culture, to some extent. Given global market trends toward greater diversity, equity, and inclusion—amplified by DEI initiatives—boardroom demographics are poised for unprecedented change. This will be game-changing, but difficult at first as boardroom cultural changes clash with boardroom politics, bringing new perspectives, challenges, and controversies.

While you cannot control how other people operate, you can take command of how you operate. And if you want to succeed at the top, focus on what you bring to the table—and meet current boardroom culture where it is.

IT'S ALL IN YOUR APPROACH

As I write this, ESG compliance is on track to become a corporate norm. We've already discussed how the financial and ecological impacts of global crises such as climate change and the COVID-19 pandemic underscore the need for meaningful action on ESG business goals.

As a result, we're seeing more sustainability committees and chief sustainability officers (CSOs) crop up in boardrooms and C-suites around the world. Companies are looking for people with ESG knowledge to lead and inform these efforts. Moving forward, expertise in sustainable business practices will become more attractive—indeed necessary—for new board candidates.

If you are female or minority, it can be argued that corporate trends toward inclusion and diversity give you an added advantage. Still, let's be realistic. If you're vying for a seat in a board of twelve, you might be considered for one or two seats; it's still very competitive to get in. And—put bluntly—you won't get a foot in the door, let alone break any established molds, with guns blazing or a victim mentality of sound and fury.

White, cisgendered man? You're not entitled to a board appointment based on these factors alone. Woman or nonbinary person of color? Listing requirement or not, you're also not entitled to a seat at the table.

At the end of the day, it's all about the value you bring, and relatability and other interpersonal skills are part of that package. In a rapidly changing world, those unable to really listen and adapt will risk forfeiting their power—whether deeply entrenched in decades of conventional business practices or rising out of newer shifts in corporate culture.

Regardless of background, each incoming director walks into a new environment with a unique culture and established set of internal politics. However—for whatever reason—people tend to underestimate politics in the boardroom, almost to the point of taboo. Too often, boards and executive leaders are not interested in meaningful change. Some just want to warm the seat, increase their own salary, and dodge board politics—even as their business operations threaten vital ecological treasures, vulnerable populations, and global economic stability.

The unfortunate truth is, some boardrooms are more contentious than others, with upper management infighting, political alliances, and cross-matrix reporting. Still, you're unlikely to hear about any of this—or if you do, to really appreciate the extent of it—until you've walked through those heavy wooden doors.

At that point, your job is not to criticize and suddenly transform the established culture, or somehow expose or otherwise "fix" entrenched toxic politics. In fact, the first order of business is simply to take stock and observe.

OBSERVATION

When incoming directors join a corporate board, they first go through an onboarding process where major company divisions from various profit centers of the company introduce themselves and their work. Generally, you'll get to meet the C-suite, perhaps C-suite minus one, and—if you're lucky—C-suite minus two.

This is your opportunity to watch and learn. You may notice clues about the personalities of different company executives and board members—for example, whether they require their secretarial staff to carry their bags or take notes for them. You can get a clear sense of pecking order based on seating arrangements. Part 3 of this book will provide a deeper understanding of these power dynamics, but for now, suffice it to say that it's best to stay quietly attentive at first.

You may not realize it, but there are a lot of different gazes on you. They know the hot button issues and internal political alliances, but you don't yet. And they're watching how you interact with everybody else for clues about your own biases and your general mode of operations. If you show your cards too early, say by vocally agreeing with a senior manager—even in casual conversation— you may inadvertently signal an alliance, causing others to write you off or decide they can't trust you. On the other hand, if you stay in quiet observation mode, you will gain valuable information.

Keeping your cards close makes it harder for people with an agenda to influence or ingratiate themselves to you. It helps you hold fast to your values and also take fuller accountability for the decisions you make—which brings me to our next point.

RADICAL (ROOTED) ACCOUNTABILITY

When I join boards, I always look to see if any of the directors have been CEOs themselves. Former and current CEOs understand what it's like to make executive decisions that impact everything from environmental impact to social responsibility— while balancing matters of shareholder interest and profitability. In short, they have experience being (sometimes fiercely) held accountable for their decisions, from all sides.

That's not to say you have to have run an entire company to be a good board director. Not at all. However, you do have to be willing and able to not only make decisions, but also accept full responsibility for the outcomes of those decisions. This may sound simple, but it's a remarkably rare skill. So many directors would rather spend a fortune on a team of outside consultants, follow their advice, then shrug and point fingers when things go awry.

While there's value in tapping outside expertise, consultants can become a (supremely expensive) crutch. And too often their perspectives receive disproportionate weight compared with those of other directors, executives, and company staff—possibly because of their often exorbitant fees, which are rarely subject to clawbacks.

DISCARD THE CONSULTANT MINDSET

Many industry consultants think they'd be ideal board members. Unfortunately, in my experience, this is frequently not the case. Being knowledgeable in your sector alone does not make you a good board member. Board members need to go beyond recommendations to make actual decisions, then deal with every consequence of those decisions.

The consultant mindset is based on providing options from an outside perspective with no real dog in the fight. Rarely are consultants in any way held responsible for the outcomes of their applied recommendations.

On the other hand, as a board member your poor decision-making can cause irreparable balance sheet company damage and get you voted out by shareholders. Executive officers are far more likely than consultants to be subject to a clawback clause, which allows the organization to reclaim your incentive or bonus funds on the grounds of poor long-term performance. Additionally, you may get trashed in the papers or even face personal litigation. In other words, be prepared to take the heat.

I'm not saying there isn't some value in occasionally tapping outside consultation. However, too many boards seem to hire consultants to avoid taking accountability. In practice, this method is risky at best. I've seen too many companies spend millions on consultancy fees, only to implement their unsound recommendations and lose millions more.

THE ART OF LISTENING (AND WHEN TO STOP)

So, how do board members make better, more sustainable decisions? For one thing, we need better discussions—and much of that comes down to listening. Not just to the people in the room reflecting your own preconceived ideas. And not because you're simply waiting for your turn to talk. Listening is the ability to genuinely consider new perspectives, especially when those differ from your own.

Unfortunately, too many board directors and executive officers struggle with this. I've sat on boards whose choices immensely impact agriculture, for example, with far-reaching environmental and social implications. Still, I too often see resistance to even consider—let alone adopt—more sustainable solutions to problems.

In the boardroom, as in life, disagreements are a given. Especially when you challenge the status quo, people get defensive; they push back. So many corporate leaders intellectually understand that their business damages the environment or mistreats workers, but they're so set in their patterns. It doesn't even occur to them to question what's always been done, to ask why, or to explore more sustainable solutions. The highest value should never be "winning" for "your side" of the argument, but having the dialogue and promoting innovation and improvement.

One exception to the rule of carefully listening to every perspective is when there's a clear conflict of interest at hand. In this situation, it's better to instead respect basic governance protocol—which not everyone wants to follow.

Indeed, some people go to great lengths to defend or deny conflicts of interest, compromising their own credibility and derailing sound decision-making in the process. For example, I once chaired a major appeals committee, which included many lawyers. Naturally, if you're a lawyer on an appeals committee, you must recuse yourself from all appeals made by companies represented by your firm.

However—you guessed it—I have seen lawyers flat-out refuse to recuse themselves from appeals processes involving companies they represent, even going so far as to vocalize opinions during the hearing in an attempt to influence other committee members. In one instance, a lawyer hurling insults had to be escorted out of the room by the very professional internal legal management team (who knew exactly what this arrogant committee member was trying to do).

Proper listening means both fully considering dissenting or dissonant points of view, and knowing when and why to stop listening. This takes practice and mindfulness to develop. It requires noticing when emotions run high and maintaining clear thinking anyway.

This is where observation skills get tested. When we're deeply invested in a topic, we often don't fully hear what the other person is saying anymore. Maybe we make assumptions and project meanings that aren't there, then we interrupt before our interlocutor can finish.

Yes, you may very well be right. But even those situations can provide insight into how people think about issues, often based on competing sources of information. To stay grounded during tense boardroom debates, it's important to accept that other people are actually entitled to different—even wrong or dangerous—points of view, and sincerely try to understand. I call this foundational empathy.

INNOVATION + WILL

Corporate leaders now realize that the exploitation model of "business as usual" has its limitations—at least *in theory* they do. Or maybe they just realize that "sustainability" has become a popular buzzword, and they want to check some boxes and slap a trendy new label on their same old operating system. Either way, you see a lot of big talk lately when it comes to ESG, but not nearly as much meaningful follow-up.

That's not because corporate leaders can't innovate. Businesses constantly adapt to new market forces. Rather, it's because we too often focus our innovation on profitability to the exclusion of all else. Sure, in theory, we'd all love to be (able to say we're) conscientious, carbon-neutral organizations that help communities while earning fat profits for shareholders. But at the end of the day, boardroom ingenuity too often aims only at that last point: short-sighted profitability.

Consider the following: You're in a board meeting where a director asserts, "We need to reduce our company's carbon footprint." You press them for details, or suggest concrete, measurable steps toward that objective, and suddenly the conversation sputters and stalls. Even if you manage to pass through some action items, executives too often surrender sustainability at the first hint of difficulty. They throw up their hands and say, "This just isn't how it's done."

I believe we can be smarter than that. We just have to match our innovation with the proper motivation. We have to be willing to forge new solutions.

I recently met a young entrepreneur, Alex Wright-Gladstein, who has managed to make ESG sustainability the guiding principle for her business. This MIT graduate co-founded Ayar Labs with the goal of cutting energy use of data in half. Their technology transmits data through light—via fiber optics—instead of electricity, which requires less efficient copper wires.

This company already puts ESG front and center. Sustainability is not some mere talking point, but rather the corporation's raison d'etre. Naturally, she wanted to integrate this approach into all facets of business, including the 401(k) she offered employees. Yet when she tried to find an affordable 401(k) without fossil fuels, she grew frustrated.

For three years, Wright-Gladstein went back and forth with major 401(k) providers, but no one was interested in developing the financial product she was looking for. At this point, no one would have blamed her for giving up. After all, her company itself helps the environment. Why nitpick about retirement funds when that's clearly "not the way things are done"? Many people would have abandoned the idea of a climate-friendly 401(k) as some untenable naive pipedream of ESG overkill.

Not Wright-Gladstein. Rather than compromise, she created

her own climate-based mutual fund, which grew into a second company called Sphere. This public benefit corporation provides financial products for companies that want to secure their employees' financial futures "without compromising on climate."

I'm hopeful that we'll see more bright sparks like this young woman who refuse to let "business as usual" curb ESG innovation. Individuals at the helm of corporations are not beholden to how it's always been done. We can demand and even innovate ESG solutions.

The problem is not lack of innovation. It's the lack of focus and will. This extends well beyond environmental matters, into the realm of social issues too. Too often, board directors and CEOs don't see a way forward on ESG issues because they simply don't care to look very hard. They're comfortable with current systems, and they don't want to rock the boat.

In situations like these, it's important to understand how corporate leaders think. Do they have vested interest in the status quo? Are they risk averse when it comes to ESG innovation, and if so, why?

FOUNDATIONAL EMPATHY

If you're interested in matters of ESG sustainability, you probably recognize the inherent value of empathy in business. For instance, perhaps you're interested in promoting fair labor practices and protecting the health and safety of both company employees and communities impacted by corporate activity.

Not everyone shares this mindset. Be prepared for situations like the one I described with the timber company willing to displace thousands of indigenous people. In Part 2, I'll share more examples of corporate resistance to responsible business practices. In these situations, don't be afraid to ask questions and calmly stand your ground when it comes to environmental and social sustainability—as well as governance issues. Often, that means choosing not to do business with an organization.

However, you should also use this empathy to better understand the culture and politics of your boardroom—as well as outside investors and business partners—that do not align with your values. Some people come in from other organizations and all they do is harp on how their last company did things. This is the opposite of listening and applying foundational empathy. We've all met people like this, and we know how challenging they can be to work with.

You can't make any positive change unless you start with basic understanding and respect for the existing culture. This requires both keen observation and research into historical and sociopolitical factors.

For example, be prepared to encounter cultural dissonance and/or misunderstanding among international business partners and stakeholders. At the very least, foundational empathy can help you remember that everyone brings a unique cultural perspective. This can help you not take things too personally if someone, for example, asks an insensitive question—like the one I fielded at the Waldorf Astoria years ago. While emotional reactivity risks alienating colleagues, responding with grace can build a bridge and promote cooperation, adaptability, and social progress.

Granted, it's also important to know your limits, and maintain a strong central ethos. I recently gave a talk in California on what I've termed "the culture of capital." When dealing with international investors, for example, you have to realize that when you get any outside investors—including foreign capital—you also get their culture. In this case, the adage "with strings attached" often holds firm.

Outside players will come in with their own perspectives. This might mean a higher tolerance for corruption or a dismissive attitude toward harmful ecological practices. If you don't have a strong ethos of what you want for your company, you may risk compromising your own ethics. Before long, the cultural influences of outside capital investors may change your own company ethos into something you no longer agree with or relate to at all.

Above all, it's imperative to remember that the culture and politics of any nation and any company—much like ESG issues—are moving targets. To thrive in the boardroom and drive sustainable growth, adaptability is key. But the trick is to adapt while maintaining both humility and integrity.

The first three chapters of this book provided an introduction to some of the cultural and political dynamics you might encounter in the changing international boardroom, and how to navigate those ever-changing forces as an ESG-minded director.

Next, in Part 2, we'll explore more deeply what's at stake when it comes to environmental, social, and governance sustainability—and discuss some major issues related to each, beginning with environmental sustainability. While my reflections here are informed by my unique cultural lens and professional experience, I hope they illuminate our global interconnectedness and add to your understanding of ESG.

ESG: WHAT'S AT STAKE

CHAPTER 4

ENVIRONMENTAL

In the mid-1990s, I traveled to Sarawak in Malaysian Borneo for a due diligence company visit on a potential investment opportunity. Due diligence involves more than just reviewing financial statements and conducting interviews; it's also the time to kick the tires, ride the motorbikes, and overall investigate the viability of material resources and infrastructure involved. The project in question was a hydroelectric embankment dam set to flood an area of Bornean rainforest approximately three times the size of Singapore.

You might recall this story from the introduction of this book. It was during this visit that I asked what would happen to the region's wildlife—some of which could not be found anywhere else on Earth—and indigenous people whose traditional lifestyle of hunting, gathering, and subsistence farming had for generations depended on this land. And it was there I was asked why I would even care, let alone ask.

The Bakun Dam would become notorious for its many false starts, delays, and lawsuits, in addition to its severe and irreversible eco-logical and social damage. By the early 2000s, the project was still incomplete, but some nine thousand native residents—including Penans, Kayans, and Kenyahs—had already been displaced from the lands they had depended on for hunting, gathering, and sub-sistence farming for generations. A timber company rumored to be quite friendly with high-level local politicians was contracted for "biomass removal." As I recall, the subsequent logging of those virgin rainforests corresponded with that same company's construction of a very large island hotel for tourists.

German-based think tank Transparency International referred to the Bakun Dam as a "monument of corruption" in its 2005 Global Corruption Report. In 2010, a documentary series on the project was banned from some local media groups. It's still hard to find clear, conclusive information on the status of this project, lending credence to claims that the entire project was a pure timber grab.

When I walked away from that due diligence company visit—and far away from involvement with the Bakun Dam project—the environmental and social consequences were not my only unan-swered questions. The company I spoke to was also unable to assure me that the technology could effectively and efficiently transmit power across such long distances via an underwater sea cable.

At the end of the day, there are other ways to produce power that don't demolish pristine, irreplaceable rainforest, disrupt miles of sea bed, and displace entire societies of people: floating solar farms, wind farms, smaller scale hydroelectric operations that don't require massive forest clearance. Considering what we're learning about the importance of rainforests for global carbon sequestration, perhaps even the burning of fossil fuels would be ecologically preferable to this massively destructive dam. But the sad truth is that this devastating project almost certainly wasn't even necessary, except maybe to build an island hotel on the cheap.

CORPORATE WILL FOR CHANGE

This wasn't the only example of extreme irresponsibility surrounding hydroelectric dams I would encounter in my career. Years after my due diligence company visit to Sarawak—after I'd launched my own asset management group—I traveled to the Philippines to speak about ESG sustainability at the Asian Development Bank. Representatives of major Asian government and private pension funds assembled there.

One topic we discussed was a series of 2005 storms that broke a hydroelectric dam in Pakistan, flooding multiple villages. It wasn't even the first time this had happened; dams in this area were notoriously unstable, especially during monsoon season. During our discussion, I asked what the government and corporate partners planned to do next. As I recall, they said, "Oh, we'll just build another dam."

This response demonstrated a flagrant lack of concern about ESG sustainability—not only by corporate entities, but by some government entities as well. As we explored in Part 1, this attitude is beginning to change for the better. However, as regulations and shareholders push for increased sustainability, we're seeing a gap in necessary boardroom expertise regarding issues like climate change and fair labor practices. In other words, many companies simply don't know how to go about changing for the better.

On one hand, this is good news for boardroom hopefuls with demonstrated ESG knowledge. Still, be forewarned—advocates for sustainable investing still face fierce resistance from corporate management, other board directors, and sometimes even government officials.

While, for example, Big Oil and Gas and their peripheral ecosystem may be the primary actors deciding whether the world will be able to meet certain environmental goalposts, they're not the only ones resistant to business innovation aimed at greater environmental, social, and governance responsibility.

In any industry boardroom, you will meet individuals who want to do things "the way they've always been done," even when that means causing preventable harm to people or nature. Sometimes, they consciously and deliberately do harm for short-sighted, self-interested reasons. Other times—more often than most people realize—they just aren't really thinking much about it. Even after board directors sign on to the concept of ESG sustainability, they often don't understand how to go about changing, and it's simply easier to stay the course.

Environmental sustainability and social sustainability are complex and constantly evolving issues. To be ESG informed means committing to a lifetime of learning and growth, staying abreast of new scientific data and exploring how environmental and social issues interconnect. Climate change, for example, is not just a matter of melting ice caps, rising sea levels, and extreme weather events. It will also significantly impact our global food supply from both land and sea and likely lead to unprecedented migrations of climate refugees.

These effects on food supply and human geography will have major implications for how we do business. And, far from anticipating and adapting to these realities, many businesses compound these same problems through deforestation, negligent waste disposal, unsustainable agricultural practices, and more.

This chapter will discuss some ecological abuses I've encountered throughout my career, such as air pollution from peat burning, mine floods caused by deforestation, and water pollution from toxic dumping. All of these disasters resulted from corporate activities, and all could be addressed through concerted action and radical accountability within the boardroom.

THE PROBLEM WITH TIMBER

As we saw with the Bakun Dam, hydroelectric power sometimes conceals an unsavory alliance with the timber industry. But even without this partnership, many tropical timber companies excel at exploitative and deceptive practices. According to research conducted by the US Agency for International Development, more than half of tropical deforestation is done illegally.

I recall one particular (now defunct) company called Aokam. Back in the 1990s, they were a darling of the stock market. Everybody wanted to own part of this company. They issued stock warrants very cheaply, and they also claimed to do sustainable replanting.

So we—I worked with AIG Investment Corporation (IC) Malaysia at the time—decided to check it out, via our usual due diligence company visits. Some colleagues and I visited a forest in a remote part of Borneo, where company representatives showed us their replanting projects. We traipsed about for hours in the forest, viewing "reforestation efforts" and boxes—all labeled and nicely stacked—purportedly full of goods to be shipped.

Of course, we didn't have Google Maps in those days. Months later, we realized they had taken us on a disorienting loop that featured the same part of the forest, over and over again from different angles. Those boxes of goods? All empty. About a year later, an investment analyst publicly reported the scam. Her report was the talk of markets across the region, particularly among global fund managers. She then received a bullet in the mail. As a result, she relocated from Malaysia to New York, and she informed many fund managers and company leaders about the threatening message.

My boss immediately called me to find out if we'd invested in the company. When I explained that we'd gotten out of the stock, but maintained a small position in the stock warrant, he said, "Get out. These people are thugs and bullies." Not long after, the house of cards fell apart: the company's stocks collapsed due to massive fraud charges.

In some ways, the business world has made tremendous progress over recent decades. Some of the ecological and especially financial abuses I witnessed earlier in my career would be unheard of now. That said, there's still deeply entrenched corruption and resistance to sustainable business practices.

Given that up to half of timber in the global market was logged illegally, the problem is not lack of laws, but rather lack of meaningful enforcement. As board members, there's not much we can do about a government's failure to enforce regulations, except to engage with the chamber of commerce or relevant industry chambers on these issues. But we can set our own course, and do our due diligence. Maintain your ESG values, and never assume your international—or even domestic—partners share those values.

The sad truth is that, in some parts of the world, people are far more likely to accept and even expect bribes. Of course, that doesn't mean you or your colleagues have to participate. It helps to set clear boundaries and expectations from the beginning about what your company will and will not tolerate.

Meanwhile, some corrupt timber companies in Southeast Asia try to justify illegal logging, arguing that given the widespread historical deforestation of the Western world, for example in Europe and North America, Southeast Asian countries should also be allowed to over-exploit their own resources. (It may be that some companies privately employ similar narratives to justify labor abuses, including outright slavery of foreign migrants—but we'll address social issues in the next chapter.)

While there is a certain schoolyard logic to this argument, it ignores the irredeemable consequences of such "business as usual"—both then and now. As we've seen, this includes the displacement and cultural genocide of indigenous peoples, extinction of irreplaceable wildlife, and dire climate change implications affecting literally everyone on the planet, which we're just beginning to fully accept.

FOSSIL FUEL HAZARDS

If you're reading this book, I'll assume you already understand the damaging environmental effects of our global over-dependence on fossil fuels. We now grasp the problem of skyrocketing carbon emissions due to human activity, so I won't belabor the point here. But climate change aside, the burning of fossil fuels comes with additional, often less appreciated human and environmental risks.

MINE FLOODS

Over the years, Southeast Asia has seen an alarming increase in floods due to constant deforestation, especially in those nations rich in natural resources, such as coal. When coal mines are built, entire communities build up around them. In recent years, people have drowned when mines and their surrounding villages become flooded or buried in mudslides following heavy rains. Tragically, death tolls sometimes include children, who both live around and sometimes even participate in mining work, often under the extremely poor safety conditions we've historically seen—and continue to see—in coal mining all over the world. As we'll discuss in the next chapter, companies too often view human life as mere collateral damage.

Floods have become an increasingly destructive theme in Southeast Asia and other parts of the world, due in large part to massive droughts followed by unusually severe rainstorms—all products of climate change caused by unchecked human activity. In fact, in December 2021, a research associate I've worked with spent fifty hours on her roof waiting to be rescued from floods in Malaysia.

I'm certainly not anti-business, and I understand that people need natural resources, such as timber, coal, and rare earth elements. But resources must be properly developed, with appropriate restrictions and both safety and sustainability policies. We must conduct our business sustainably, with a mind to the future and to all stakeholders (everywhere).

As corporate leaders, this means developing a system of controlled development, with a mind to renewal, conservation, and community safety. Especially as rainfall in Southeast Asia continues to increase, we cannot simply destroy topsoil with explosives or hastily construct a mining shaft, then throw up our hands when the monsoon floods pour in. We also cannot assume that ESG values—or indeed, local laws—will be honored when doing business with foreign partners. Due diligence and supply chain transparency by conscientious corporations are key.

TRANSPORTATION OF FOSSIL FUELS

While people may be aware of the environmental and social hazards of fossil fuel extraction methods like dirty coal mining, they rarely discuss issues of transporting these materials. Remember the story I told in the introduction about my very first boardroom meeting? The centerpiece of that ad hoc meeting's agenda was literally a ship *on fire*.

Since not all nations have coal and natural gas in their own country, they have to import fossil fuels, typically to run their power plants. Sourcing, shipping, and using combustible materials like coal, oil, and natural gas means risking, well, *combustion*. In other words, your fossil fuel business can quite literally blow up in your face—and history provides ample proof: from the Kuwait oil fires to the Guadalajara sewer explosion to mining and shipping explosions all over the world. Such literal blowups greatly impact company boards, supply chains, commodity prices, and other geopolitical consequences around the world.

HAZE FROM PEAT BURNING

About 10 percent of Indonesia consists of peatland, an important part of the ecosystem that helps regulate the water table and absorb heavy monsoon rains. This swampy peatland soil contains high levels of partially decomposed, highly combustible carbon-rich material. When drained, bricks of peat can even be harvested and burned for fuel, as some Northern European countries have done.

In Indonesia, peat often burns not for fuel, but to clear land for plantations. When palm oil and wood pulp companies expand plantations, they often either drain peatlands or intentionally (and illegally) set fire to mangroves rich with peat-rich soil by pouring diesel over the land and lighting it. When peat ignites, it can smolder (up to fifteen feet underground) until a thick, slow-burning haze envelops the air for hundreds of miles around, impacting multiple countries across the region.

The resulting haze often proves deadly, and to an astonishing degree. In 2015—a particularly devastating year for peatland fires—researchers from both Harvard and Columbia Universities estimate that more than one hundred thousand people died from the effects of breathing peat haze in Indonesia and neighboring countries.

When peat haze spreads across Indonesia and into Southeast countries like Singapore and Malaysia, it not only impacts public health, it also closes schools, shuts down businesses, and slows economic growth. In short, society cannot function properly as no one can venture outside. Meanwhile, this agricultural burning destroys peatlands rich in endangered biodiversity.

In one of the many roles I served in pushing sustainability

throughout the region, I suggested the regional stock exchanges should impose modest fines—less than $4,000—for board directors of regional companies that allow deliberate peatland burning. I spoke to board chairs, directors, and CEOs across Southeast Asia. Not one institutional authority would agree to even this small fine, apparently preferring to protect the directors of their listed companies and plantations.

Unfortunately, unlike in the United States, China, Taiwan, Korea, and some other nations, we don't have systems in Southeast Asia allowing small investors to arrange class action suits against errant directors or corporate management. In this part of the world, we must depend on regulators. If regulating authorities ignore, defend, or even protect corporations whose practices destroy our lands and harm our people, we need to think what else can be done.

Government authorities in Southeast Asia can be very slow to act. In fact, some reports claim that Indonesian government officials underestimate the toll on both environmental and public health to an obscene degree. Indonesia's official death toll from the 2015 haze was a suspiciously far cry from the more than one hundred thousand deaths reported by Harvard and Columbia researchers.

Until we get brutally honest about the ghastly, widespread impact and corporate causes of peat burning, regional governments' claims to ramp up enforcement of existing rules on peat burning ring hollow.

TOXIC DUMPING AND WATER POLLUTION

Sometimes, as with mine floods and deadly haze, environmental abuses by corporations are impossible to ignore. Other times, they can go undetected for quite some time. But that doesn't make their impact less dangerous. One example of this is when companies dump toxic materials, typically into rivers and oceans.

These days it seems that everything comes wrapped in plastic—and much of it cannot be dumped in certain places. As a result, wealthier nations tend to send their plastic waste to Southeast Asia, where it gets dumped in the ocean or landfills. Make no mistake—despite the PR rhetoric, plastic is not easily recycled at all. Still, it's a ubiquitous part of product packaging all over the world.

Ocean dumping has been an ongoing problem in our part of the world—and it's hardly limited to plastics. As a rescue scuba diver in the mid-1980s, I witnessed firsthand extensive damage from dynamite fishing and waste dumping in Southeast Asia's coastal waters. Decades ago, I met an American entrepreneur whose company shipped used car batteries across the Pacific for the purpose of dumping battery acid into the sea near Korea and selling leftover metals for scrap. Based on the suits he wore and the cars he drove, this man made very good money on the enterprise too.

Similarly, companies previously dumped toxic materials such as mercury and lead from old television sets. In 2022, the Taiwanese Supreme Court awarded US$1.82 million in damages to the plaintiffs of a class action lawsuit against Radio Corporation of America. The case involves dangerous practices at a Taoyuan factory dating back to the early 1980s, such as workers forced to apply toxic solvents without personal protective equipment (PPE) or proper air circulation. The company also dumped toxic TV parts underground, contaminating local soils and nearby drinking wells.

General Electric took over RCA in 1986 and sold the Taoyuan factory to Thomson Consumer Electronics in 1988. Three years later, Thomson shut the factory down, after discovering severe pollution issues. In 1998, a group of workers began organizing lawsuits, leading to several investigations that confirmed that dangerous levels of toxic, carcinogenic exposure directly correlated to the former employees' cancer diagnoses. Still, it wasn't until decades later that accountability prevailed through legal means.

CHICKEN FARM WASTE

Luckily, we've seen some progress when it comes to regulations and enforcement surrounding electronics disposal. Still, pollution of water—our most precious natural resource—remains a serious issue. Everything from fertilizers and pesticides to landfill waste can leach into drinking (clean water supply) water.

One example from Malaysia involves poultry farming. Many Malaysian chicken farms line rivers that flow into Singapore. These chicken farmers transfer massive volumes of chicken feces into a storage area for composting. The resulting waste water is transferred into an aerated lagoon, which builds up over time to cause sludge bulking. Essentially, this occurs when excess incoming sludge overflows into nearby rivers, dangerously contaminating human drinking water. When rain levels are low, the ammonia levels from chicken waste sometimes build up in the river water beyond what water treatment plants can handle.

My asset management firm became aware of the issue during our due diligence visits to water companies. We found shockingly high levels of ammonia in water treatment plants downstream from chicken farms. Sometimes, ammonia levels got so high, the plants had to shut down until rain came to help dilute the toxicity.

Although dumping toxins like chicken waste into rivers is technically illegal, the negligible fines—less than US$200—do little to deter company workers. Unfortunately, people are also willing to bribe regulation officers, many of whom are underpaid and willing to accept.

Even our vast oceans have been deeply impacted by corporate laziness and greed. From toxic waste to pervasive plastics, our oceans have long been seen as a dumping ground for human spoils. Combine this with rampant overfishing using dynamite and trawling methods, and we're on track to threaten some of the world's largest and most valuable ecosystems—which includes our own food supplies.

FOOD SUPPLY

As I write this, we're experiencing such supply chain crises all over the world, whether due to lingering effects of the coronavirus pandemic, the impact of Russia's Ukraine invasion, or something else.

To protect their domestic markets from supply issues, Pakistan and Indonesia have planted more olive and palm trees and reduced exports of oil and palm oil, respectively. Vietnam is similarly reducing rice and fruit exports as concerns mount about future food security. Such patterns contribute to inflation and other destabilizing economic trends around the world, as well as risk of famine.

But while pandemics and wars both come and go, climate

change—and its impact on food supply—is set to persist and worsen—unless we start making some serious, concerted changes.

One example relates to El Nino, the less frequent, warmer phase of southern Pacific Ocean temperature oscillations. For years, climate scientists have reported (to many deaf ears) that rising global temperatures have made El Nino events more intense. Although the phenomenon is a natural part of the ocean cycle, climate change has made El Nino events even warmer—and more destructive—than usual, bringing prolonged droughts and ravaging farms and fisheries alike.

During recent El Nino cycles, the Philippine Department of Agriculture initiated water management and production support programs for farmers, installing division dams and other small water projects. One particularly devastating effect of the more intense weather patterns has to do with rice supplies in the region.

In the Philippines, as in many countries, rice is an essential staple of the national diet. Even today, a bag of rice is often included in employment contracts. Indeed, I personally know a Philippine entrepreneur whose chicken rice cafes struggled to scale until he decided to offer all-you-can-eat rice along with his signature chicken dish. He made a calculated bet that the typical local consumer will only eat up to three bowls of rice in one sitting. As a result of that move, business boomed into a widespread restaurant chain he eventually sold for nearly $400 million—which illustrates the cultural and economic value placed on rice within this region.

Though essential in the fight against global hunger, rice is also a vulnerable crop requiring enormous amounts of fresh, clean water.

I remember how the 1997 El Nino drought impacted seventy-four thousand hectares of agricultural land in eighteen provinces in the Philippines. That same year, I sat in a board meeting with a young fund manager who suggested it might be a good speculation tactic to buy rice and dump it, thereby manipulating market prices in the company's favor—during a massive drought, when people were literally starving. Needless to say, I was appalled.

This is what I mean when I say that, as corporate leaders and global stakeholders in a shared future, we can and must do better.

SOLUTIONS AND ALTERNATIVES

Throughout the twentieth and early twenty-first centuries, corporate leaders could easily ignore environmental concerns about harmful business practices—and even ridicule their critics as irrelevant "tree huggers."

Recently, environmental advocates have expanded in both numbers and clout to include international regulating bodies such as the United Nations, as well as influential investors, advocacy groups, and pension fund managers—plus an exponentially growing number of everyday consumers who, thanks to the digital age, are much more aware of the stakes.

It's harder than ever for board directors to isolate themselves in luxury and ignore these trends toward ESG accountability. Increasingly, corporate leaders realize that natural environments and human communities, such as those that thrived in Bornean rainforests before the proposed construction of unnecessary hydroelectric dams, are invaluable in and of themselves—and indeed, something we *all* should care about.

Granted, too much about the fate of our planet still rests on decisions regarding fossil fuels made by very few, very powerful individuals behind closed boardroom doors. That said, corporations and individuals everywhere can influence matters by making better decisions about how we conduct business and consume products.

As board directors and company executives, I believe it is our moral imperative to lead the charge in long-term ESG sustainability, and take radical accountability. A company's niche footprint might involve anything from exploring cleaner energy sources and replacing plastic with recycled and recyclable materials to implementing more sustainable agriculture standards to help secure domestic food supply. Meanwhile, as individuals, we can personally adjust our lifestyles by choosing to buy organic foods, renewable energy, and recycled/recyclable materials when possible.

TRACKING GREENHOUSE GAS EMISSIONS

In 2001, the World Resources Institute (WRI) and the World Business Council for Sustainable Development (WBCSD) brought together a group of stakeholders from corporations, NGOs, and others to figure out how businesses can best track their emissions. The results have standardized corporate metrics for tracking emissions around the world.

Their Greenhouse Gas Protocol divides into three categories: scopes one, two, and three. Scope one covers direct greenhouse gas (GHG) emissions made by company operations like factories and vehicles. Scope two includes indirect emissions from a company's purchased electricity, steam, heating, and cooling. These two are very easy to calculate.

Scope three gets a bit more complicated. This accounts for all the indirect emissions resulting from a company's upstream and downstream value chain activities. It involves everything from employee commuting to purchased goods and services, all the way to emissions caused by consumer use of a company's products. This one's trickier to calculate, but certainly not impossible.

At the moment, we now have international standards for companies to follow regarding all three emissions scopes. Companies everywhere are gently encouraged to declare where they are on these emission standards. That said, pollution laws vary greatly from country to country, and calculation metrics (imperial vs. metric) differ as well, making both enforceability and true standardization difficult.

ALTERNATIVE ENERGY

The COP26 UN Climate Change Conference focused heavily on green energy sources. It's interesting to watch as governments and corporate leaders sift through the political and economic interests surrounding various alternative energies, such as nuclear power and hydrogen technologies—both controversial methods at best with dicey political and ecological implications.

Then again, no alternative energy source comes entirely free of debate. Wind farms produce loud booming sounds that annoy nearby residents, and they're often accused of decimating bird populations. However, organizations in the US point out that the impact of wind turbines on bird populations pales in comparison to other hazards. The US Fish and Wildlife service reported in 2017 that wind farms killed more than 230,000 birds. However, electrocutions, poison, and collisions against cars and buildings accounted for millions of bird deaths. Domestic and feral cats topped the list, responsible for an astonishing estimated 2.4 billion bird deaths.

One of the fastest growing—and to me, most exciting—segments of renewable energy is solar. Homeowners and businesses enjoy tremendous energy savings and much reduced carbon emissions through the use of solar panels, and I'd love to see more government tax incentives, for both industry players and consumers, encouraging this technology.

Speaking of government action, former British Prime Minister Boris Johnson announced in 2020 that the UK will ban the sale of new petrol- and diesel-powered cars beginning in 2030. Initiatives such as this will impact the resale value of such vehicles, further influencing people to either invest in electric vehicles or opt for alternatives such as public transport or bicycle commute.

In 2021, Denmark's Maersk—the world's largest container shipping company—announced its plan to move to "green methanol," which it claims will help the company achieve carbon neutrality and cut a million tons of carbon dioxide emissions every year. Maersk invested about US$1.4 billion into methanol-powered vessels built by South Korea's Hyundai Heavy Industries. However, a year later, Maersk reported ongoing difficulty in securing sufficient green fuel to power the fleet. Company officials aim to get at least some methanol-powered ships in operation by either 2024 or 2025.

It will be interesting to see how wildly fluctuating gas and oil prices affect consumer habits and values. For example, in parts of Southeast Asia, while vehicle prices remain prohibitively high, governments subsidize lower-grade petrol, which stabilizes its cost. Meanwhile, in the US and other places where cars are more affordable, drivers must pay actual market prices set by WTI or Brent oil markets. This makes consumers painfully conscious of the cost and volatility of our global fossil fuel dependency. The pandemic already changed the world's commuting habits, as more workers maintain remote work. Hopefully, we will also see a higher consumer demand for electric vehicles (with higher battery capacity), mass transportation, and safe bicycle infrastructure.

ENVIRONMENTAL SUSTAINABILITY AS A SOCIAL ISSUE

Recently, when governments and corporations talk about environmentally sustainable investing, they focus mainly on energy and climate change. However, climate impact is profoundly interconnected with ocean health, food security, and other issues poised to gain importance in coming years and decades. And, as we've seen in this chapter, environmental issues are so often inextricably linked to matters of social responsibility.

You cannot talk about land development or ocean usage without discussing the impact on native peoples whose way of life depends on those natural habitats. Likewise, reckless dynamite mining strategies, desertification, and deforestation increase flood risks, toxic dumping poisons drinking water, and peat burning presents terrifying public health risks.

In the next chapter, we'll look more closely at these public issues, along with social sustainability related to corporate labor practices; employee health, safety, and well-being; and digital responsibility.

CHAPTER 5

SOCIAL SUSTAINABILITY

If your family members were among communities or workers directly impacted by your choices in the boardroom, how would you perceive the situation? This question can be applied to nearly all matters of corporate social sustainability. Still, many companies never bother to ask.

Like environmental and governance issues, social sustainability—the "S" of ESG—evolves with the times and often collides with corporate, national, and global culture and politics. In Part 1, we addressed matters related to diversity, equity, and inclusion among board directors, as well as community impact. This chapter will discuss additional social sustainability issues, such as workers' rights, labor abuses, health and safety, and digital responsibility.

For sustainable corporate success, companies must reconcile a healthy bottom line with how they treat human beings. Not only because it's the right thing to do, but also because our growing digital connectivity makes it increasingly difficult for corporations to get away with reckless treatment of workers, consumers, and communities. As we'll see in this chapter, board directors can either hold themselves accountable and become leaders in social sustainability, or be held accountable by others.

MODERN SLAVERY AND LABOR ABUSES

One particularly egregious recent example of labor abuse involves modern slavery among Thai fishing fleets on the high seas of Indonesia. In 2014 and 2015, the Associated Press published exposés revealing this human trafficking of enslaved fishermen, mostly from Myanmar, who had been lured in by agents and subagents under false pretenses of paid work.

The AP report described men chained and sold for as little as US$420, kept in cages, regularly beaten, and forced to work 20+ hour shifts for little to no pay. Sources claimed that those attempting to escape were routinely shot and thrown to sea. AP investigators snuck cameras onto the Indonesian island of Benjina to interview the captive fishermen. They also tracked a single shipment of the seafood caught by enslaved workers—first by satellite and then on the ground in the United States.

What they found was an astonishingly opaque and complex distribution system involving dozens of factories, markets, and storage plants. Slave-caught seafood was getting mixed in with other products both in Southeast Asia before shipment, and on the ground in buying nations, such as the US, UK, and Europe. This Byzantine structure and process made it difficult for an individual restaurant, supermarket chain, or, say, pet food company to even know whether their supply chain indirectly supports and profits from slave labor.

Difficult, but not impossible.

During our Corston-Smith company visits, we began asking hypermarkets (which combine supermarkets and department stores) if they bought seafood from fishing companies connected to forced labor and slavery. Their responses tended to be evasive claims that they didn't know the "culture" of their supply chains. However, as a result of slavery and other migrant abuses, the price of prawns and other seafood delicacies dropped sharply in buying countries, though few retailers or consumers even took the first step of asking why.

Many large, publicly listed companies were implicated in the AP report. This led to calls for boycotts among activist groups in the US, UK, and Europe, as well as immense pressure from shareholders of both listed and unlisted supermarkets and hyper-markets to investigate seafood supply chains. Some of the fishing companies involved released statements promising supply chain audits and claiming newfound commitments to ensuring that workers receive fair wages and safe working conditions.

As a result of this press, the US State Department downgraded Thailand and other countries in the Association of Southeast Asian Nations to a Tier 3 trafficking designation in 2014.

LABOR ABUSES

Human trafficking and enslavement represent extreme examples, but labor abuses vary widely. For example, certain fast fashion textile companies have claimed they didn't know their overseas factories employed school-age children. In most parts of the US, UK, and Europe, for example, such a thing would never happen, but in parts of Asia, some workers bring their children to work. For one thing, they may not have access to safe or affordable childcare, but parents also may see this as a way to train their children in the workforce and involve another pair of hands.

In a profoundly interconnected, digital world, all it takes is a few photos of such labor abuses to put a company at risk. From fishermen in Southeast Asia to coffee plantations in Brazil to migrant workers in the USA, it's harder than ever to hide bad behavior. If basic human decency doesn't inspire your fellow board directors to demand supply chain transparency, they might consider the monetary implications of things like class action lawsuits, errant factories getting closed down, and disruptions in major supply chains.

I recently spoke with C-suite executives who expressed outrage and near disgust after the US Customs and Border Protection (CBP) confiscated their company's PPE equipment. They claimed the CBP wields excessive power and fails to follow proper processes, and that a single photograph—which may be altered—results in confiscation of their products.

I replied that the US CBP has become more strict because, for too long, manufacturers of PPE have failed to take responsibility for counterfeit, unapproved, or otherwise substandard products. The tolerance for such practices among authorities in large markets like the US and EU has understandably decreased. If they don't like the security protocols and quality controls, perhaps they should find a more permissive market.

HEALTH AND SAFETY

Inking relationships with international partners complicates matters of social responsibility and transparency because board directors must account for labor practices throughout their supply chain. You may recall that tumultuous first board meeting I described in this book's introduction. In addition to a ship on fire, that board meeting addressed multiple tragedies related to health and safety failures along its production lines.

One issue related to new construction cranes the company had purchased. Previously, they used cranes from companies that provided skilled technicians along with their machines to properly train port operators. However, when the company decided to order much taller cranes from a new foreign manufacturer, not only did they not send personnel to train workers, but the instruction manuals were only written in a language no one at the local port could understand. As a result of improper safety training, many accidents occurred. At one point, a crane operator lost control over his machine, two cranes collided, and a worker fell from a crane cabin meters high to his death.

In a subsequent meeting, we discussed the death of a port operator who drove an unauthorized passenger car onto a pontoon. When the driver's boot got stuck on the accelerator, the car drove straight off the pontoon and sank. Unable to dislodge his foot from the boot stuck under the pedal, the operator drowned.

These tragic incidents cast light on the dangerous negligence involved in the company's port operations. For one thing, there were no official health and safety standards related to who could drive onto the pontoon, which vehicles were permitted, or under what circumstances. Furthermore, there was clearly no security staff enforcing standards or supervising the situation—a stunning oversight considering that both an elementary school and naval operation were situated near the port. Indeed, around that same time, a shipping logistics truck overtaking another vehicle around a blind bend accidentally struck and killed children at a school crosswalk near the port entrance.

Obviously, no board directors want preventable deaths occurring on their watch. These tragedies resulted not from deliberate misbehavior, like toxic dumping or forced labor, but from preventable oversights related to worker health and safety—for example, assuming new cranes would come with proper safety training, or at least instructions that workers could read. As a result, we didn't think to question whether workers had the proper tools to conduct safety test runs within a controlled framework. It certainly didn't help matters that the board consisted of many new directors not yet fully briefed on company activities, and everyone was distracted by hostile board politics.

Awful situations like these really do occur—and they serve as wake-up calls to all involved that social sustainability is not just a matter of ticking boxes. It may quite literally represent a matter of life or death.

PROTECTING COMPANY EMPLOYEES

Years later, while serving as chair of a board, I had to address a previous incident involving an employee who had been assaulted. The assault incident occurred when someone on a motorbike broke the glass window of our employee's vehicle and attacked him as he drove home from work. Because this man served in an investigative capacity for our company, there were many reasons to conclude that the attack was almost certainly directly related to his work.

The man endured permanent, debilitating injuries, which severely impacted his family finances. Despite all this, his immediate supervisor was now suggesting we cut the man's health coverage to avoid paying his medical bills related to the attack, claiming that his treatment was taking too long.

It turns out they'd opted for the minimum basic insurance coverage to save on monthly premiums. The idea was that, because employees were mostly young, they would only pay occasional out-of-pocket expenses. Unfortunately, all people can get sick and hurt. As such, not only did this approach not save the company any money, it also incentivized cruelly abandoning workers should they suffer serious illness or injury. This same company deducted bonuses from workers forced to take more than a few days of sick leave—in a country prone to Dengue Fever, which requires seven to ten days convalescence.

Disgusted by the suggestion of halting this man's insurance policy, I encouraged the board to discuss the fairness we owed to the employee, which I felt included protecting his access to company medical coverage. On a positive note, I learned that one of the directors had privately visited the employee at the hospital. Still, I soon caught wind of a similar event in which two workers were threatened with the same modus operandi: motorbikes circling their vehicles as they drove home from work. Was this another planned attack? These workers only reported the incident after I asked to speak to them about unrelated issues. Astonishingly, their supervisor argued against "escalating" this information by informing the CEO.

In response, we implemented administrative changes to help protect the identities of our employees. For example, letters sent to errant companies previously included the names of investigating officers. We changed that to include only division information. These days, videoconferencing technology also allows such employees to work remotely, reducing dangers presented by public commutes.

The two workers threatened with potential physical harm resisted my calls for full-time security until I made clear that the protection was as much for the company as for them. What's more, nobody wanted to make a police report. I nevertheless reported the incidents to the heads of police and the anti-corruption agency.

This incident came in stark contrast to the treatment I'd received early in my career as a young fund manager at AIG (IC) Malaysia. Maurice (Hank) Greenberg, then the chair and CEO of AIG, found out via my senior boss in Hong Kong that my sister had contracted colon cancer while working as a UN physician in Bosnia. He responded by arranging for her to be transferred from the UK and treated at Sloan Kettering. She declined, but the generosity of this offer deeply impacted me, emphasizing that leadership goes far deeper than merely pushing for the bottom line. Foundational empathy resonates throughout the culture of a company when strongly modeled by top leadership.

At the very least, when faced with a similar incident regarding the safety of employees, more responsible companies would have ensured sufficient medical insurance coverage, immediately implemented full-time security tracking, and even arranged for psychological support to help staff cope with the dreadful events.

STAFF HARASSMENT

Sometimes health and safety issues relate to dynamics among company staff. Another issue I faced as board chair related to patterns of harassment reported by a staff member. This particular individual initially posted about the mistreatment online under an alias—let's call them "Sal"—before directly emailing me about the situation, and eventually meeting me in person.

Sal's Glassdoor posts claimed that their direct supervisor systematically alienated them by restricting them from meetings and promoting their juniors above them. While this may seem like subjective hearsay, the posts also alleged that the supervisor daily screamed at Sal and others and subjected them to such intense verbal abuse that they suffered high levels of psychological and physical stress. The undeniably high employee attrition rates under that supervisor appeared to align with these letters and Glassdoor reviews.

This example helps underscore how digital connectivity and documentation can expose issues related to health, safety, and employee treatment within an organization. One quick Google search, and people can view anonymous employee reviews about company culture.

Meanwhile, workers publicly compare notes on social media platforms like LinkedIn and Glassdoor. The point is that employees are increasingly holding corporations accountable for how they treat people. At the end of the day, foundational empathy and social responsibility are what both draw and retain top talent while cultivating a culture of caring for your company.

DIGITAL RESPONSIBILITY

It's remarkable how much of our lives gets mediated by screens—that is, by algorithms and digital codes that remain inscrutable to most of us, even as they profoundly influence our lives, opinions, and mental health.

In 2021, a former Facebook employee testified to the US Senate Commerce Subcommittee on Consumer Protection regarding her former employer. She made the case for government regulation of social media platforms on the grounds of safety concerns.

Specifically, she leaked internal research, conducted by Meta (Facebook), finding that 13.5% of teenage girls reported that Instagram use worsened their suicidal thoughts and 17% felt the platform contributed to their eating disorders.

One wonders if the board members of this company were aware of the potentially dangerous effects of its algorithms. Had board members questioned management on the issue, especially as dependency on social media grows? Or do they turn a blind eye to such concerns, preferring instead to focus on rising share prices?

Perhaps Meta's original intention was not to deliberately cause mental anguish among teenagers. However, upon discovering the problem, to downplay rather than resolve the issue *is* a deliberate choice. Choosing to double down on a business model shown to likely harm vulnerable young people makes it very difficult to claim any concern about ESG sustainability in business.

It's easy to see how social media platforms, from Meta to Twitter to TikTok, need to contend with digital responsibility. However, all companies should be asking questions about how their digital presence impacts consumers and community members, from the algorithms involved in platforms where they advertise to cyber-security and data protection. According to the UK Information Commissioner's Office, Facebook violated data protection laws by allowing companies like Cambridge Analytica to harvest the personal data of millions of its users worldwide without their consent.

REMOTE WORK

In 2020, professionals all around the world were forced to almost instantly adapt to working from home. From my experience, the banking sector took data security measures quite seriously, providing secure devices and sometimes even having an IT professional set up employees' work technology at home. However, not every company had the resources or foresight to maintain cybersecurity standards for remote workers.

Among the risks are unsecure home network connections or use of public Wi-Fi. Workers also—too often—have difficulty spotting scams and phishing attempts. They may use weak passwords or fail to encrypt files. To make matters worse, oversharing on social media platforms makes it easy for hackers to mine personal information.

Make sure you trust your company's technological support, and that they properly train all of your staff to spot scams and reduce vulnerabilities—for example, plugging pen drives on office devices within a dedicated pen drive workstation to avoid data theft, which we've done at Corston-Smith since 2015. This is to protect clients' data (portfolio data as well as fund flows). Beyond that, it's also important to have analog backup systems and brick-

and-mortar solutions, just in case digital access gets threatened. For example, staff should have strategic access to landlines and primary information within safely kept paper files.

Like all social sustainability issues, digital responsibility is a rapidly evolving topic that board directors cannot ignore. Indeed, most companies now have a Chief Technology Officer, and increasing numbers of boards have IT committees. I believe this is a move in the right direction, provided that those directors populating IT committees have actual firsthand knowledge of the technological issues. (Another suggestion is to have a specialist individual invited to be part of a special projects team. Normally this is outside of the board committee but just targeted on a specific large IT project.) Otherwise, a board may end up going the route of hiring IT consultants, deepening their dependence on costly outside support with zero accountability. At the very least, I'd recommend appointing an IT specialist to a special projects team targeting major IT projects.

Those of you old enough to remember Y2K may recall the unfounded terror and dread surrounding the notion that corporate data could be irrevocably lost. This represented a nightmare for capital market participants dealing with financial products maturing after 1999, such as insurance policies, long-dated debt instruments, exercise prices for warrants, or corporate entitlements. Many companies spent a fortune on digital goods and services to save themselves from a crisis that turned out to be a false—perhaps even manufactured false—alarm.

So what can we learn from things like the Y2K fiasco, or pandemic-related WFH risks? What's going to be the next tech crisis to worry about? I'm certainly not the topic expert to answer these questions, but as a veteran fund manager and seasoned board director and chair, I do understand the social implications of matters like data protection and algorithm ethics—and the value of appointing real subject matter experts to your board or to a specific committee, rather than outsourcing this issue to unaccountable consultants.

DEFINING STAKEHOLDERS AND COMMUNITY

This chapter on social sustainability began with the example of enslaved fisherman in Southeast Asian countries. Perhaps that seems like a remote or extreme example that has nothing to do with your leadership journey. However, in our interconnected world, one must stay vigilant and ask questions to ensure that labor abuses don't occur far down the foreign supply chain—or even right under our noses, through unchecked staff harassment or digital mismanagement.

The golden growth years for the ASEAN region, peaking by the late 1990s, were largely based on widely available abused and forced labor. These days, international legislation requires corporations to take more accountability. For example, the UK Modern Slavery Act of 2015 demands that organizations with an annual turnover of at least 36 million sterling publicly report the steps they're taking to identify and prevent modern slavery in their operations and supply chains.

Meanwhile, we still see overworked, poorly compensated migrant workers everywhere. At the beginning of the COVID-19 outbreak, I saw firsthand how migrant workers in the region were rounded up and, in some cases, literally chained by their feet with their hands tied behind their heads. I suspect some were undocumented, and I'm not sure whether they expected to be vaccinated or shipped home, but it certainly looked like I was witnessing prisoners of war.

As we've seen, social issues related to ESG vary widely—from human trafficking and lesser labor abuses to staff harassment to digital responsibility. When it comes to each of these issues, corporate leaders must adopt a zero tolerance policy for those that bring shame to our markets. Every life matters—not only those on fat payrolls overseeing your company's bottom line.

To me, it's very telling how a company describes their relationship with the people off their direct payroll who are nevertheless affected by their business activities. For example, when discussing the areas hosting their businesses, do they refer to "our" host community? Do they include themselves as a part of that system? Or do they refer to them as people in *that* community *over there*? This small difference may well determine how a company engages with and invests in the areas where they do business.

We cannot on one hand condemn abuse of our own children, then enable it among other communities. Besides, with increased digital connectivity, supply chain transparency is getting easier. Not only that, but the risk of exposure is greater than ever. We can no longer throw up our hands and claim innocence because "we didn't know."

When board directors truly embrace the idea that we are all stakeholders—including their workers on the ground and the communities affected by their business—they will view business through the lens of accountability. This is the corporate version of the golden rule, and to me, it's the crux of social responsibility in business.

CHAPTER 6

GOVERNANCE

Some years ago, while serving as a board chair, I was on a personal trip for my daughters' swimming competition when I received a Friday evening after-market call regarding an urgent transaction worth hundreds of millions of dollars with a foreign company. Senior management were sending round a directors' circular resolution, or DCR, to immediately push through the deal. This occurs when board members receive a document via circulation and are expected to sign a resolution on a matter if they agree with the details outlined in the document, rather than passing it at a convened directors meeting. That is, with no in-person board discussion.

DCRs can be convenient for simple, procedural decisions, perhaps regarding a new detail on something previously discussed and agreed to by management and the board. For example, reviewing a customary terms update on a banking facility or minor change in approval limits or authorization rules. However, DCRs should not be used to resolve controversial or urgent matters unfamiliar to directors.

This instance was anything but customary and minor. Just imagine blindly signing off on a transaction involving hundreds of millions on a Friday night, while out of town. The company secretary next informed me that a corporate lawyer on our board was refusing to sign the DCR due to incorrect banking details in the attached document.

"I'm not comfortable with this, so I won't be signing either—not until the banking details are clearly stated," I said. Instead—despite furious objections by senior management, pressured by the urgent timeline, management called round to lobby other directors to sign the DCR.

Meanwhile, I called the president of the foreign company to request two additional days to work out and include the correct payment details. I explained to him that I didn't necessarily have ethical or fiscal objections to the deal, aside from the fact that we needed correct documentation to safeguard both institutions. I also postponed the matter until Monday when proper information could be sorted out, then sent follow-up emails for an audit trail.

I later learned about a similar banking oversight of a related party transaction, which, due to haste and pressure, hadn't been reported by our audit committee. I requested a direct inquiry into the process flow of this deal, from end to end. I'm not sure that ever happened. Years later, when the company in question was investigated by the US SEC for potential breaches of the US Foreign Corrupt Practices Act, I was hardly surprised.

This story emphasizes the (time) pressures you may face as a board member—and the fact that you do not have to bend to them. Abrupt, hurried circulating resolutions like this one, while perhaps not always nefarious, do represent a major red flag. Hasty deals under pressure too often sacrifice transparency and due diligence. It doesn't help when those board directors most keen on loosening protocol seem both particularly friendly with management and lacking in relevant subject expertise.

When you serve on a board, you have to watch yourself, even—perhaps especially—when interested parties assure you that, despite clear audit issues, everything's "just fine." You will deal with ethically compromised directors—perhaps even your internal lawyers. Meanwhile, external legal counsel will never abide being rushed, because they'd be liable if something were amiss. It's increasingly likely that you'd be liable as well, but we'll get to that in a moment.

TRANSPARENCY OF PROCESS

The first two chapters of Part 2 discussed what's at stake in terms of environmental and social sustainability. However, every single one of those issues—and much more besides—is rooted in governance. As I learned from launching and leading the asset management firm Corston-Smith, environmental and social sustainability in business requires proper governance structures and procedures.

What do I mean by "proper governance"? The simple answer is transparency of process. Without transparent processes, you can end up with meaningless greenwashing and box-ticking, combined with corner-cutting, corruption, even outright fraud. You won't know how decisions were made in the past or who is allowed to make them, and you won't know how to make better decisions moving forward.

The growing global focus on ESG sustainability has led to a lot of greenwashing. Companies love to claim they're becoming more ESG compliant, but often their targets are vague, and they lack the robust, transparent plans or metrics needed to achieve these goals.

For example, company directors may talk about carbon emissions. Perhaps they promise to conduct more remote video calls, requiring less air travel—but they fail to formalize specific plans or track progress through quantitative analysis. Whereas, another business may calculate their GHG scopes 1–3 and take concrete steps, such as signing up for a sustainable travel partners program with an airline, which enables businesses to transparently assess and reduce their travel footprint.

Certainly ESG sustainability requires more than skipping the occasional flight. Board members should also examine how the companies and suppliers they do business with address ESG issues like climate, fair labor, or digital responsibility—for example, whether they adhere to science-backed, measurable climate targets, document their adoption of labor practices, or publicly disclose how they develop algorithms for digital engagement.

There's a lot at stake when it comes to governance, and how governance intersects with environmental and social sustainability. On the legal side, this chapter will discuss increasing liability for independent board directors and deferred prosecution agreements over matters ranging from corruption to foreign labor abuses down the supply chain. In terms of market dynamics, we'll look at how ESG issues affect listing requirements and indices in stock markets, as well as sustainability-linked financing.

Healthy governance requires transparency at every level and

degree of the international commerce ecosystem. Market regulators must set clear, measurable guidelines for investors to know how to properly and sustainably invest in markets. Meanwhile, brokerage firms, analyst reports, and mutual fund companies must promote ESG products to investors with documented evidence to back up claims, and sustainability-linked lenders should be clear about ESG key performance indicators required to secure lower interest rates.

Finally, as board directors and executive leaders, our decision-making must have transparent documentation and metrics consistent with stated goals and compliant with laws and regulations. This not only empowers board leadership and aligns corporate goals, it also protects directors from legal action—where this chapter's discussion begins.

There is a broad range of corporate bad behavior, from subtle toxic habits to flagrant abuse. If you lack clear procedures for and documentation of decision-making, you may inadvertently condone the antics of bad actors—and as we'll now explore, that could make you, as a board director, personally exposed to legal action.

CLASS ACTION LAWSUITS

In the United States, as in many countries, shareholders can join together to sue companies, including independent board directors, for misappropriation of funds and other bad behavior. For example, if you're investing on behalf of a US 401(k) retirement fund (an employment-based plan that allows tax-preferred withdrawals for retirees who contributed), you must follow guidelines put in place by the Employment Retirement Investment Security Act, or ERISA—or risk lawsuits.

Other places in the world, companies still get away with all manner of abuse and corruption, mainly because of obstacles to collective action. However, that seems to be changing. Let's look at one major example in Asia.

CHINA CRACKS DOWN ON FRAUD

As mentioned in Chapter 1, 2021 saw the first collective investment action suit against a Chinese corporation when more than fifty-five thousand shareholders won a court-ordered payout of approximately USD$385 million.

Most notably, the company's former board chair, vice chair, and several other executives and independent directors were found personally liable for the systematic fraud. The court sentenced the chair to twelve years in jail and fined him for manipulating the stock market, failing to disclose material information, and bribery.

Previously, board director fines for misconduct were capped at USD$94,000. Revisions to China's Securities Law in 2020 changed the penalty to up to 50 percent of all the ill-gotten gains. All five independent directors on the board of this company—most of them academics—were held personally liable for between 5 and 10 percent of the total US$4.8 billion reflected in the company's cash balance overstatement.

Initially, the company blamed the cash balance overstatement on an accounting error. Then it was discovered that false transaction records were connected to the company's misreporting. Suddenly these directors—pulling in annual board fees of only around $31,000—were looking at personal fines up to $19 million.

This outcome was not only a big win for shareholders, it also sent shock waves through boardrooms across Asia and around the world. The message? Independent directors can no longer so easily ignore, tolerate, or even claim ignorance of fraudulent activities.

Many independent directors in Asia will openly admit they're not truly independent—that they lack sufficient autonomy in carrying out their rules. Meanwhile, I've seen more than my share of will-fully obtuse directors who don't show up or read the minutes, but nevertheless condone or ignore dubious practices. When sitting on a board, directors must make a good faith effort to improve the execution of fiduciary duties and properly analyze company processes and declarations made to all stakeholders and regula-tors. Board directors must do their part to uphold the integrity of the institution despite pressure from political masters.

In other words, becoming a board member simply to collect fees and a free lunch is quickly becoming less glamorous. Indeed, in the wake of this ruling, twenty Chinese companies announced mass resignations of their independent directors. In a culture that tends to publicly withhold motivations for leaving a board, most of them cited "personal reasons."

LIABILITY FOR FOREIGN LABOR ABUSE

As I write this, the UK subsidiary of an Asian PPE manufacturer is set to proceed to a full judicial hearing for labor abuse charges. This is the first high court case in the UK to address modern slav-ery in the UK supply chain. That it's occurring on the tail end of the coronavirus pandemic shows that corporations can no longer turn a blind eye to ESG abuses—not even during a global crisis.

Meanwhile, in spring 2022, the European Commission announced it will soon introduce a legal instrument to ban products linked to forced labor and child labor from the European Union's internal market. This gives the internal trade committee of the European Parliament plenty to do as they determine how best to monitor forced labor in value chains.

DEFERRED PROSECUTION AGREEMENTS

Allowing investors to come together for collective, or class action, suits against corporate leaders sends a strong message to bad actors, which can help curb transgressions and stabilize markets. Otherwise, investors rely on national regulators, who may, in some cases, be compromised.

However, court cases can become long, drawn-out, and costly affairs. As such, many corporations negotiate a deferred prosecution agreement, or DPA, instead.

A DPA occurs when a company has been formally charged with a financial crime, often bribery or fraud, and to avoid disrupting business operations with a messy, time-intensive trial, the company signs a contractual agreement with the government agency such as the US SEC or DOJ. Many other countries—the UK, France, Canada, and Japan, for example—have also developed DPAs.

Rather than arguing their case in court, a company can sign a DPA, then agree to pay a fine, disclose relevant information, and follow strict guidelines and restrictions to clean up their act, under very close monitoring. When corporate leaders sign a DPA, this indicates they agree to both the charges and the terms of compliance or remediation—down to every last comma on the page.

If you spend time on major international corporate boards, you likely will deal with a DPA at some point. It may even come as an unwelcome legacy surprise following a merger and acquisition of another company. In fact, I experienced this firsthand with a company that acquired a smaller business only to later discover that the acquisition was coming under federal investigation regarding its own foreign business dealings.

The process was quite destabilizing and nerve-wracking. A US federal appointed monitor arrived at our offices with dozens of staff to conduct interviews and sort through thousands of documents. If they found any evidence that we'd breached the terms of this DPA, the company might not be allowed to clear or conduct business with US dollars, which would make it a pariah of global commerce.

Furthermore, according to our lawyers, if anyone on the board or staff said anything that implied negligence, we might be held personally liable—and if so, we'd be on our own. "Get yourself a good lawyer," we were told. Keep in mind that director liability insurance covers you as a director for some things, but not everything.

DPAs can be very thorough processes that uncover trails of corruption through corporate supply chains around the world. As a result of a DPA, your company may be required to stop doing business with "politically exposed persons" (PEP) and "politically exposed corporations" (PEC) implicated in the charges. This could include closing down corporate branches, breaking ties with clients, and firing staff involved in the criminal activity. Of course, you also have to pay hefty fines and cooperate with federal monitors.

In short, operating under a DPA is not considered "business as usual." Or at least, it shouldn't be.

Then again, what's acceptable in "business as usual" certainly has evolved over time. Until 1977, when US legislators pushed through the Foreign Corrupt Practices Act (FCPA), companies could more easily get away with bribery, sometimes quite flagrantly earmarking funds for corrupt purposes. Before this law, the practice of openly paying an incentive to get a deal done was rampant, especially within foreign ventures.

Now, in the early twenty-first century, cross-border enforcement agencies often collaborate to pursue evidence of criminal activity. For example, in a recent high-profile DPA involving a European aerospace corporation, the US Department of Justice, the UK Serious Fraud Office, and the French National Financial Prosecutor (PNF) worked together for eight years to investigate the company and serve a DPA.

DPAs can have a freezing effect on business, as potential clients or partners shy away from evidence of corruption. However, this is not always the case. Recently, a well-known global telecom giant entered into a DPA with the United States Department of Justice. By signing the agreement, the company essentially admitted to undertaking a campaign of corruption in five Asian countries to solidify its grip on the telecommunication business—yet they continue to conduct widespread business.

The DPA exposed evidence of third-party agents and consultants associated with this telecom company paying bribes to government officials and managing off-the-book slush funds. Agents set up sham contracts, paid pursuant to false invoices and improperly accounted for in the books and records.

The telecom company also completed a draft due diligence report that failed to disclose the spousal relationship between the owner of the consulting company and one of the high-ranking government officials. Millions of dollars flowed through a subsidiary company to various agents, consultants, and service providers through gifts and travel entertainment for foreign officials, including customers from state-owned telecom companies.

In 2021, the DOJ determined that this particular telecom company breached its obligations under the DPA by failing to provide certain documents and factual information. Still, despite essentially agreeing to these charges and even *breaching* terms of the DPA, the telecom company in question continues to dominate in the region—even signing deals as a 5G single supplier for some Southeast Asian countries.

Despite their continued command over the region, the DPA did cost this company over a billion dollars in combined penalties, which at least sends a warning message to other corrupt global corporations and their partners.

If you're a board member or aspiring director, be prepared to potentially deal with a DPA—even if you're indirectly implicated through an M&A or by unwittingly conducting business with a compromised corporation.

ESG AWARDS AND SCORECARDS

We've now seen how anti-corruption legislation, lawsuits, and DPAs can help keep corporations above board—and otherwise expose their transgressions. Beyond these legal obligations, most companies must also create detailed annual reports with sustainability sections.

Plus, everyone must abide by company incorporation rules and stock market listing rules. Meanwhile, governance codes or policies developed by national or international associations, such as the European Corporate Governance Institute or the United States Corporate Governance Code, may represent best practices to follow, though they remain unenforceable.

Many countries instead offer awards or scorecards to incentivize meeting governance codes and best practices. Companies then hold up awards or scorecards as bragging rights. Unfortunately, though, fraud does occur, sometimes causing awards or high governance scores to be given erroneously.

I remember a company in India that received the Golden Peacock governance award, issued by the Institute of Directors. Eventually, it came out that the two brothers running the company had accountants create fictitious accounts, and they didn't disclose important material facts. Their accountants ended up going to jail, and the award was rescinded. The board directors claimed to be unaware of the fraud.

In other words, these awards are not proof of good behavior. They can be given based on unverified, incorrect information, or their methodology for rating ESG sustainability may be less than robust or transparent. In that way, they can be quite similar to market indices.

(STOCK) MARKET INDICES

There are many different kinds of stock market indices. An entire market itself—like the S&P 500 or the Dow Jones—can be built as an index, for example. Whole market indices tend to be more transparent in terms of rules and regulations and how those are enforced through listing requirements, metrics, corporate disclosures, and penalties.

There are also specific indices categorized by sector or theme, such as a healthcare index or ESG index. Although I agree with the principle behind these "for good" indices, too often very dubious companies somehow make the cut, and there's little transparency of process in determining which companies make the cut. Sometimes specific indices have clear criteria—you must have a certain percentage of earnings from a certain sector, for example, or meet stipulations regarding board size, demographic constitution of the board, or percentage of stock liquidity. Other times, less so. This can lead to misleading indexation at best. At worst, it opens the potential for deliberate market manipulation.

Many fund managers or Exchange Traded Funds (ETFs) will use an index as a benchmark for promoting their fund management product to investors. For example, the MSCI Emerging Market Index is very popular in my part of the world. Companies will fight tooth and nail to get into that index to become attractive to ETFs.

Many fund managers buy (or sell) everything on an index. This is called passive fund management. Whereas active investors, such as those managing hedge funds or active ETFs, pick and choose individual stocks, passive investors buying or selling index tracking funds and passive ETFs aren't stock picking. They're not following up on every company in the index to verify that they're performing well or following regulations, then adjusting their portfolios accordingly. Instead, they simply buy or sell shares of the entire index to gain or reduce exposure to certain kinds of stocks. As a result of widespread passive investing, huge fund flows tend to follow companies included in these index listings.

Remember that big class action lawsuit in China? This was not any old unknown company that had misled investors, but a company regularly included in one of the most widely followed indices.

Inclusion in indices can greatly benefit companies. If a particular stock gets included in an index, more money flows into that stock or that market. Likewise, if your 401(k) invests in the 2022 ESG index, the companies included in that index benefit from your 401(k). On the other hand, if a company is removed from an index, it will generally see massive selling.

So, how do indices like, for example, the S&P ESG, determine which companies to include? Part of the answer is that companies are rated against other companies within their particular sector. So oil companies get compared to other oil companies, and the ones that perform best according to the S&P ESG scorecard get included in the ESG index. This could result in, for example, an oil company getting included on this ESG index. That company may seem relatively sustainable compared to other oil companies because they're doing substantially more than these competitors to offset their carbon emissions. But compared to, say, a fintech company, the company would measure quite differently.

Some critics have also pointed out biases in the S&P's criteria for ESG. Notably, the index ratings do not look at scope three carbon emissions, which result from use of a company's products. Instead, they only consider greenhouse gas emissions from company operations. As a result, the far more important bigger picture gets lost. The index ends up giving disproportionate credit to some companies, while underrecognizing contributions other companies have made toward environmental sustainability.

Granted, company management cannot mistreat workers or violate governance codes without those issues impacting their ESG index rating—simply because, for example, they make electric cars. But would these matters warrant wholesale exclusion from the ESG index? We need to apply some proportion, and we need more transparency and discussion surrounding these indices. For example, we don't know whether environmental, social, and governance issues get weighted differently.

For the sake of comparison, let's look at the Dow Jones Sustainability Index, which for years has included a Malaysian company that makes PPE. This allows that company bragging rights about meeting the criteria for a sustainability index.

Meanwhile, their products have literally been banned in the UK and the USA because of labor abuses. Not small ones—or even moderately large issues like allegations of racial discrimination. People have literally died in the factories. Workers have been forced to sleep in the factories, squatting six people to a bed. They're working excessive hours without fair wages under deplorable conditions—and this company gets listed in the Dow Jones Sustainability Index.

However much I believe we need sustainability indices, they too often lack fair metrics and overall transparency. We want companies to be sustainable and responsible. But what message does the market send when one company makes the cut for an ESG index even as their products are confiscated due to egregious labor abuses while, meanwhile, a leading electric car company is dropped from an ESG index due to comparably minor social issues?

Ignoring these questions invites potential market manipulation. These indices have huge influence over where money flows through the market—and we're talking billions. Hypothetically, if powerful individuals who determine the criteria for these indices decide they don't want more money flowing into one stock price, for example, they could technically manipulate the index criteria accordingly, by taking advantage of the "subjective" part of the rating process.

Every time these indices are updated, about twice a year, investors rebalance their own portfolio percentages, causing huge turnovers in the market. When the value, known as market capitalization, of a stock goes up, that stock ranks higher. Investors managing value-weighted ETFs respond by adjusting the number of shares they own within the index in proportion to those shares' relative overall value. So if stock A and stock B start off with equal market capitalization, then stock B's value doubles, these investors will buy more shares of stock B, causing even more money (value) to pour into it—and vice versa; stock prices fall due to index devaluation or exclusion from an index—a self-fulfilling prophecy of money chasing money.

This is why the creation of indices should be as transparent as possible, with little to no subjective element. The market would be better off with clear weightings for environmental, social, and governance categories regardless of sector. Too many global market participants just want to buy index funds and passive ETFs, as these represent low entry or exit fees, which provides them exposure to a theme or sector or entire stock market.

SUSTAINABILITY-LINKED FINANCING

In addition to transparency of process, sustainable governance means staying abreast of ESG regulations, targets, trends, and opportunities. It also means introducing specific, measurable KPIs for environmental and social responsibility into your operations, and investigating ways to offset or minimize any costs involved with becoming more ESG compliant.

One way to do this is to take advantage of sustainability-linked financing. These are debt securities that can be raised by investment houses that lend or provide funding to companies demonstrating high standards in environmental, social, and governance sustainability.

There are so-called "green bonds," which are instruments for financing or refinancing environmentally friendly practices. There's also a growing interest in raising "blue bonds" relating specifically to ocean and water health—protecting coral reefs, setting more responsible fishing standards, and the like.

Finally, you can also find floating-rate ESG sustainability bonds, which provide companies with specific key performance targets. If companies achieve these environmental, social, or governance KPIs, they will pay a lower interest rate to the issuing financial institution.

For example, to qualify for lower rates in a floating ESG sustainability debt instrument or bond, it's not enough to say, "We're reducing our carbon footprint through Zoom meetings." Instead, you must calculate that reduction and show proof of lower GHG emissions to qualify for a lower interest rate, typically recalculated annually. Plus, they tend to have a clawback feature: if, after qualifying for the lower rate your GHG emissions metrics change for the worse, you must repay the difference in interest rates for the time period in question.

Even when investing in unlisted companies, the private equity fund manager operating with ESG sustainability bonds has to incorporate ESG-based covenants into the structure. That might mean, for example, restricting foreign direct investments (FDIs) made with funds raised from the ESG sustainability instruments in countries or companies failing to comply with certain ESG standards.

While such market incentives certainly help, I believe the tipping point will come once we see stricter, enforceable international accounting standards, international legislation, and stock market listing requirements related to ESG sustainability. Noncompliance gets quite expensive, causing corporations to quickly fall in line.

RADICAL ACCOUNTABILITY IN GOVERNANCE

As governance and sustainability issues become more enforceable via regulations, abuses may get more subtle or hidden. It's vital to recognize toxic cultural and political boardroom practices at every level, as early as possible—and to do what you can to align your company's operations with sustainable practices.

All of these issues can get complex at times, but ESG sustainability culture doesn't have to be overwhelming. You don't need to win an award or hire a consultant to tell you what looks good based on current trends in ESG sustainability indices. Such insincere efforts too often devolve into meaningless greenwashing or governance accolades. At its simplest, ESG sustainability in governance can just mean setting broad sustainability structures and goals your company believes in and can achieve, with realistic timelines and scenario planning—then actually pursuing those goals.

When companies cynically adhere to standards and requirements without actually believing in ESG sustainability, the results get depressing. For example, you see companies and countries with poor emissions performances collaborating with companies and countries with a better carbon footprint to offset their damage. In their minds, piggybacking on someone else's ESG sustainability efforts means that nothing has to change within their own operations.

However, the truth is that things do have to change. We cannot keep decimating rainforests and flooding entire regions for cheap timber for hotels. We can't use coal-fired plants in perpetuity without becoming a stranded asset in the future, or reopen old mines without even utilizing technical data such as the JORC Code. Business strategies like that are not only destructive, but they're purely short-sighted, unstable, and, well, *unsustainable*.

Similarly, we cannot continue to tolerate foreign labor abuses. The practice is not only profoundly inhumane, it's also not worth the legal and financial risk of exposure. We already have satellite imaging that can monitor the movement of workers to gauge their hours, or literally track the supply chain of products developed by forced labor around the world. Between eyes in the sky, smartphones in everyone's hands, and social media connecting us all, no longer can corporate leaders so easily exploit, lie, and avoid public outcry (that leads to boycotts of the company's products).

Sustainable governance takes many forms. It could mean more transparent supply chain audits to avoid implicating your company in modern slavery. Maybe you begin measuring your company's carbon footprint according to scope metrics, or raise more debt through ESG sustainable bonds. It could also mean something as banal as refusing to sign a potentially problematic DCR, despite fierce pressure from management.

Now that you better understand what's at stake in environmental, social, and governance sustainability, it's time for Part 3. The final section of this book provides a deeper dive into how to become an agent for change in the boardroom. This means navigating boardroom politics and culture; interpreting everything from audit trails to seating arrangements; leveraging leadership opportunities; and more effectively engaging with all stakeholders.

AGENTS FOR CHANGE

CHAPTER 7

A SLEUTHING GUIDE

If you ask Merriam-Webster, "politics" means a lot of things, mostly to do with government, of course. But one final definition they give is this: "relations or conduct in a particular area of experience..." The first example provided? "*Office* politics."

Are we even surprised?

If there's one thing everyone knows about politicians, it's this: they like to say one thing, then do something entirely different. The same is unfortunately true within the corporate boardroom—particularly when cultures collide.

There's no doubt that, in the boardroom, cultures are colliding. Hopefully, this results in companies listening more closely to all stakeholders. This book began examining how boardrooms around the world are beginning to shift from an Exploitation Model to what I call an Accountability Model, evidenced by growing adoption of ESG sustainability measures in business (or at least by a lot of big chatter about it).

As a result, boardroom demographics stand on the cusp of major change, as director seats open to historically underrepresented groups, including those with ESG expertise. Part 1 ended with an introductory guide to the boardroom for new, sustainability-minded directors, focusing mainly on mindset and the importance of observation.

Now that (in Part 2) we've addressed pressing ESG issues, risks, and opportunities related to ESG sustainability, let's return to the dynamics of the boardroom itself.

The sad truth is that—like actual politicians—board directors too often say one thing and do quite another, misrepresenting intentions and motivations, concealing misdeeds, dominating discussions, and even intimidating those who don't agree.

Part 3 will provide concrete tips on how to deal with such nonsense, starting with practical advice for new directors seeking to understand board dynamics, as well as insights into both leadership and the art of stakeholder engagement.

To begin, this chapter offers an in-depth sleuthing guide: what to read, how to observe, whom to talk to, and overall how to analyze boardroom documents and dynamics to better understand your organization—which may include identifying red flags.

Ready? Let's approach those boardroom doors and get to it.

APPOINTMENTS

Before we talk about onboarding, I'd like to address those aspiring board members for whom those doors never seem to open.

In recent years, I've seen an increasing number of groups offer training programs—especially for women and other groups traditionally underrepresented in boardrooms.

Beware of any group claiming some ability to get you onto a corporate board. While they may be able to help explain board structure or improve your own "board readiness," no one but the company itself can guarantee you a board position.

So how do board appointments work, anyway? Most boards work with headhunters that assess the board composition and look for someone to complement the existing skill matrix.

They will follow certain guidelines. For example, the chair of a remuneration and/or nomination committee must be an independent director, or the chair of an audit committee must have a certain level of demonstrable experience in finance. Finally, if you are in a regulated industry, any appointment to that board must be approved by the authority, such as the US Treasury, federal reserve, or US SEC.

Speaking of government authorities, be careful about joining the board of directors of any state-owned enterprise (SOE). Well-known examples of this in the US include publicly traded, government-sponsored commercial mortgage companies Freddie Mac and Fannie Mae. Serving on the board of an SOE can get you flagged as a politically exposed person (PEP), restricting your ability to join other boards, particularly those of international corporations. In addition, elected officials and other high-profile public figures are also considered PEPs. All aspiring and current board directors should stay abreast of the latest screening requirements and corporate restrictions for both PEPs and politically exposed corporations (PECs).

That said, many board candidates get referred by current board members and influential staff. In other words, it's still very much about who you know. In most countries, major shareholders nominate board members—even so-called independent directors, casting doubts on their independence—to represent them on the board, especially if the shareholder in question owns more than 50 percent of shares.

I personally know exceptionally qualified women, with decades of senior experience working all over the world, who struggle to break into the boardroom—despite joining women's groups and high-profile board training programs. While these groups may offer some value, the most important resource remains your own ability to network and ask for introductions.

Be mindful of which boards you agree to serve on. If you get invited to serve on a board, research your future fellow board members, management team, and major shareholders before accepting. You don't want to lose your own credibility by associating yourself with thuggery or money launderers. While this may sound extreme, I have seen a longtime leader of the Chinese organized crime triad become a chair of a publicly listed company—soon after his release from fourteen years in prison, and despite making the US Office of Assets Control's List of Specially Designated Nationals, which includes terrorists, narcotics traffickers, and other high-profile criminals barred from doing business with US persons.

FIRST THINGS

When you've been appointed to a new board, the first order of business is: who's who.

Spend some time learning about your fellow board members. What are their skillsets and competencies? What kind of corporate experience and/or expertise do they bring? Who sits on and chairs which committees and for how long? Are any committee chairs due for rotation? Also, find out whether these members sit on other boards or companies together or previously worked in the same institution. This will give you a very basic understanding of overall dynamics, including the independence and clout of each board member.

Next, pour over the company organizational chart to get to know your company's management and staff structure. How many divisions make up the whole? Who heads each department? What does each team do, and how does it all intersect? Focus first on memorizing the C-level suite, plus lower-ranking managers once or twice removed from this top-level executive team (C-level minus one or two). Next, examine which divisions contribute the most in terms of top line and net earnings to the company. These typically represent the heavyweight divisions in terms of influence and demand on resources.

During onboarding, you'll get a chance to meet major players and learn about their respective divisions and teams—but trust me, things get confusing very quickly. Spending time with the organizational chart in advance will help you more meaningfully engage with management.

One person in particular will prove invaluable, in terms of both information and ease of transition, and that's the company secretary or cosec team. This team typically comprises a main registered legal company secretary, sometimes with a support team that takes minutes, plans meetings, and provides legal support. We'll go more into that role and relationship in a later section, but for now, suffice it to say that building trust and rapport with the cosec is worth more than gold.

Speaking of the cosec, they may request your CV or bio for a press release. If so, I advise that you ask to review the draft press release before it goes out. You may well send your curriculum vitae to the cosec only to have it edited without your approval. Then, when it's published in the media, it looks quite different.

To share a personal example of this, I once saw removed from my bio all references to my firm's Diversity in the Boardroom report, which has shaped considerable positive change for women in the region, including a federal government aim in Malaysia to encourage a 30 percent goal for representing women on leading corporate boards. This personal victory had been edited out of my bio by some anonymous individual on the board—likely a director or senior executive averse to this degree of women participation on corporate boards.

At first I was even more frustrated that the cosec wouldn't reveal who had done this, but of course she was being professional. A good cosec is a master of diplomacy and discretion, who avoids pitting board members against one another. Besides, it's important to pick your battles, conserve your energy, and start off on the right foot.

As I said, during onboarding, you may spend two or three days with other new board members sitting through management presentations. If you can read the right company documents beforehand, you'll be able to not only better follow along, but also to discern who is accurately representing themselves and their department.

WHAT TO READ

In other words, do your homework. In this section, I'll give you a list of key documents to request in advance of onboarding, plus tips on how to analyze and interpret them—both during onboarding and throughout the course of your board tenure. While many board members slack on this—indeed some hardly even glance at active meeting agendas—understanding the history and operations of your company will help you better serve and guide your views.

In addition to identifying key paperwork, this chapter will advise you on how to navigate company archives; analyze what you find, both qualitatively and quantitatively; and cross-reference documents for helpful information and patterns.

COMPANY CONSTITUTION OR MEMORANDUM OF ARTICLES

First up is the company constitution or memorandum of articles. This will give you a good sense of institutional history, strategy, and vision.

I recommend you settle in and have a long, uninterrupted read of this document as it provides insight into founding principles and established precedents informing your company's governance. From the constitution, you'll be able to appreciate your institution's origin story, including how it was founded. This will help you understand what you can and can't change and shed some light on how and why the company was set on its path—and whether/how it may have since strayed from these original principles.

BOARD CHARTER AND AUTHORITY MANUAL

The board charter is a policy document clearly defining the respective roles, responsibilities, and authority of board directors. It essentially clarifies what the board can and cannot do in terms of directing and guiding company management.

You should also have access to authority or approval limits listed in a manual, with a focus on limits for each rank of staff within company management. This resource might tell you, for example, whether and to what extent the CEO can approve levels of payment or proposals without informing the board meeting. Reviewing this document helps you understand where you may need some increased checks and balances. Because these are living documents, always ask when the last changes were made to either the board charter or the authority manual.

For example, I once dealt with a situation where the CEO of a publicly listed company changed the authority manual to ensure he could personally hire every single person in the organization—except for the C-suite people—to ensure control over and loyalty from the entire organization. This permitted him to hire and fire as he pleased below the top management team. As a result the board lost all power of oversight regarding which staff were moved, underpaid, overpaid, or treated as sacred.

BOARD COMMITTEE TERMS OF REFERENCE (TOR)

The board committee terms of reference functions like a board charter, but takes a more focused look at board committees. It outlines the size, members sufficient to meet quorum, required skills and experience, responsibilities, limitations, and overall scope of each committee. For example, the terms of reference for the audit committee may specify that the chair of the audit committee must have experience in finance.

Sometimes the TOR includes meeting dates for each committee. Audit committees tend to meet more often, while remuneration and nomination committees usually only meet when the company reviews staff KPIs, exits, succession planning, organizational structure, or pay scales.

MATTERS RESERVED FOR THE BOARD

From the company secretary, you should receive a document listing "matters reserved for the board." In every company, certain decisions cannot be made by executive management; they must have board approval. Matters of material impact on a company or its subsidiaries are normally reserved for the board. For example, board approval may be required before increasing company debt or share capital (which dilutes everyone's shareholding), or creating encumbrances of the company. Or, in a company jointly owned by two partners, the document may stipulate that one owner cannot sell the company unilaterally without board approval.

OFFSITE AND STRATEGY MEETINGS

Once you have a grasp of the company's governance structure and related documents, request the meeting minutes and reports from company offsite and strategy meetings. These tend to be great resources for bigger-picture understanding and research.

Strategy meetings occur when the board and key management all go off site for a few days to a week. These retreats tend to be more relaxed affairs allowing corporate leaders to think outside the box, brainstorm issues, and discuss strategy, typically for the next year. Often, they invite companies to present in specific areas of interest, regarding either routine business or potential opportunities.

The offsite strategy meeting is also where you identify core problems, brainstorm solutions, and set timelines and goals for scenario planning. The questions addressed at an offsite depend on the metrics and challenges of the company. Let's say revenues are consistently down. What does the company need to do to drive business? Are there manufacturing or delivery issues? Are there issues with a product's market fit? Where should the company go from here?

I tend to ask for the last three years of offsite/strategy documents. This provides a sense of broad goals, key issues, and strategic plans. It's also helpful to compare these documents to the company constitution or memorandum of articles to see if the year-to-year master plan aligns with the vision, mission, and values of the company founders/leaders.

Sometimes, you can spot trends right away from offsite documents. For example, I've seen evidence that management presents the same or nearly identical proposals, multiple years in a row with seemingly no progress made. This suggests a disconnect, perhaps between good intentions and the will, resources, or cooperation needed to actually follow through.

You might also detect conspicuous omissions of the key areas. Perhaps issues related to digital responsibility or to environmental sustainability simply never come up. This might warrant further investigation of how those areas are commonly dealt with, and why they're not considered a priority. It could be that everything's fine on that front and/or there are more pressing matters at hand. On the contrary, there may be improper reasons why management wants to avoid certain topics, or simply a lack of appreciation of their importance.

BOARD EVALUATION

Once every year or two, boards often have what we call a board evaluation exercise (BEE). Typically this entails "anonymous" ratings of board members, by board members. Ideally, these assessments are conducted by an objective, professional third-party entity.

Reading these assessments can reveal quite a lot about internal politics and power dynamics. For example, they may describe which board members try to dominate discussions and decision-making.

One thing to note is that these evaluations often are not anonymous to the cosec. This emphasizes the importance of having a professional—that is, diplomatic, neutral, and discreet—cosec; otherwise, BEEs can devolve into antagonism and divisiveness.

MINUTES

We've come to my favorite part: meeting minutes. I cannot emphasize enough the value of looking over past meeting minutes, and cross-referencing with the documents mentioned above. (There's so much to unpack that the next chapter, on board leadership, will return to this topic in more depth.)

Unlike the company constitution or strategy meeting reports, ordinary meeting minutes are less concerned with aspirational vision and more reflective of actual day-to-day operational priorities and challenges. This is the down-and-dirty account of company affairs.

How far back to go largely depends on both how problematic your board is and whether your board convenes quarterly or monthly. If meetings are quarterly, you can go back up to five years. If monthly, I'd start with two or three. Review these chronologically for a clear understanding of how key issues and board dynamics have progressed over time.

Bear in mind that you do not have to read every line of these board meeting notes beginning-to-end before your onboarding. Just a skim of the past few meetings will help you navigate those early interactions, while also revealing recurrent issues that warrant more focused, strategic research. Make sure you note which individuals or teams are linked to these recurring issues or projects. While they're not necessarily in the wrong, you should be aware of which people and teams are in the hot seat.

For example, if, after speaking to the head of legal, you find out the board has ongoing cases, check the minutes for anything related to those matters. Generally, you'll be able to request a digital copy with a search function where you can type in a certain name or issue.

You're also looking for patterns suggesting both problems and strategy. Are there ongoing discrepancies between the stated goals and timelines of scenario planning and their execution? Which key issues keep coming up? Maybe there's a high staff attrition rate in specific departments that never seems to resolve. This indicates chronically low morale and warrants further investigation into which teams and departments experience the most turnover and why.

If you read carefully, you may be able to discern whether certain board directors try to protect potentially implicated staff from scrutiny, versus board directors keen on learning more about potential problems. Do some individuals try to distract from, diminish, or table certain discussions? If the minutes are recorded properly, you can often glean which board members promote greater transparency. If you encounter potential red flag issues in the minutes, strike up a casual chat with the cosec or minute taker to see if you glean a more nuanced understanding of what happened.

You may also see a trend when it comes to hires, appointments, or terminations. Maybe there's a clear trend of senior staff, particularly the nomination committee, allowing certain senior players to always hire friends or family members. Whatever the case, make a list of any behavioral or cultural issues that keep coming up in meeting notes over the past few years.

Matters Arising

Finally, pay extra attention to the part of the minutes called "matters arising." These are items raised in the board meeting that require CEO or executive management response to questions and potential follow-up. Look for updates in subsequent meetings' matters arising. If management is trying to circumvent the board on these issues, for example, you may see a pattern of nobody following up or responding to either meeting questions or relevant emails.

For example, the chair may ask for a breakdown of key areas on scorecards for staff KPIs, which generally drive performance and accountability. Management keeps promising to do this before the next meeting then coming back with nothing. If this is not something the board keeps a close eye on—say the chair doesn't want to call attention to it, or the cosec gets careless—such unresolved issues can end up dropped from meetings altogether.

Board Committee Minutes

You should have access to minutes from board committee meetings and special subject matter or task force or direct inquiry (DI) subcommittee meetings as well. These offer a great resource for assessing the follow-up on key issues. A good committee chair will verbally report at the board meeting and distribute a summary sheet reporting their board committee findings and recommendations to the board at every meeting. You may notice that some committees (typically audit committees) brief the main board and submit extremely detailed reports, while others' reports seem conspicuously lean or cryptic. This can suggest deliberate concealment or other ethical red flags; other times, it's just common laziness.

OBSERVATION TIPS

As I pointed out in Chapter 3, the best thing to do at first is to keep your own counsel and keenly observe. As you're busy researching and evaluating your company operations, other people are meanwhile evaluating you—and sometimes they try to pull you into alliances and agendas.

WATCH AND LISTEN

Your first impression does not have to make a big splash. Don't worry about asserting your viewpoints just to take up air time or to compete with other people. Remember that you already made it in the door; you don't have to prove yourself at your first meeting.

Now is the time to hold your cards close, while establishing and maintaining lines of communication. Often, before adjourning, the chair will go around the room and ask for final comments or issues to be raised from each director. As this is your first meeting, now is your time to offer innocuous observations, or simply say that you enjoyed meeting everyone and learning more about board matters.

Especially early on, people will try to draw personal connections: "Oh! We both attended the same school," or "We've worked with the same colleague." Maybe they'll drop hints that they personally know a regulator or industry leader to ensure you know they are linked with strong cables to the top.

Some may go as far as to obtain your work—or even personal— phone number and send direct messages, or they may see you at an event and bombard you. I was once approached by a C-suite manager eager to discuss business matters—as I sat at a wedding with my husband. My husband politely suggested we put away the shop talk and enjoy the reception, but this individual wouldn't take the hint.

Some management may attempt to shamelessly gossip to poison the well against certain other individuals. I recall one example of a C-suite executive talking to me about a work issue and then suddenly bringing up a C-suite colleague, alluding to this person's spouse as a crook. I was horrified that this individual would smear a colleague like that in an attempt to get one up against them.

When it comes to discretion and confidentiality, do not for one moment believe in the sanctity of the boardroom. In extreme cases (such as one I personally experienced as a board member while that company engaged in a tense, global court case), directors may even find surveillance "bugs" in the boardroom itself. While this level of digital surveillance is rare, sensitive information can and does escape the boardroom.

This is particularly true when it comes to garden variety gossip. Whatever corporate leadership perceives about you will trickle through the rest of the organization. This doesn't have to be ominous—sometimes the information is even complimentary, and typically everyone's just trying to protect their own interests. But the truth remains: information about what you say and how you behave will spread.

For example, if you respond calmly and firmly to disruptive or inappropriate behavior—as I managed to do during the espresso machine debacle I related in Chapter 2—it will show that you stand (and stand your ground) for what is right. As a result, people may be more likely to share information with you about what's not working in the organization.

BOARDROOM BEHAVIOR

When you first walk into the boardroom, pay close attention to where everyone sits at the boardroom table. Generally, the cosec determines who sits where, and their choices tend to reflect power hierarchies as well as internal rifts and alliances.

Obviously, seats on either side of the board chair are reserved for the most senior roles, such as the CEO, or maybe representatives for majority shareholders or the senior independent director. Beyond that, you may find the cosec separates directors or management with known rivalries or disputes, as well as allies who noisily converse with one another during meetings.

Prepare yourself for bad behavior. Just because you've breached the pinnacle of corporate leadership does not mean you will always be dealing with mature, rational grown-ups. In the boardroom, you may very well see childish whispering and snickering among directors, even while someone is presenting on a contentious issue. With smartphones, you may even see directors clearly texting each other across the room. (Although, for highly confidential meetings, be prepared for the cosec to ask for all smartphones to be left in the basket outside the boardroom.)

I have certainly been on boards with excellent management teams who work very well together. But there is always some level of political friction between them, as well. Over time, you may notice entitled directors, domineering "alpha" personalities, and even outright bullies. Pay attention to how board directors and the C-suite leaders treat the cosec—who expects the cosec to carry their bags, for example. Some board members may act aggressively toward the cosec, chair, and other directors, cutting people off and sometimes even shouting over someone who is giving their opinion or in the middle of a presentation.

I have been in a room where one board member pointed to three individuals and announced, "I'm worth more money than all of you combined." On another board, a major shareholder once suggested a director put their house up for sale, "because you're going to need extra money when I start suing you."

In other words, boardrooms are not all glamor with board fees and free lunches. This work can be very hostile, and you need to keep your wits about you.

Even in a relatively civil boardroom, there's so much to glean from non-verbal cues. For example, pay attention to how different board members respond to different topics. Perhaps a conversation about labor abuses comes up and you see certain individuals seem to scoff or dismiss the issue. (This underscores the disadvantage of remote digital meetings, where it's harder to read into people's body language.)

If you have good board leadership, the chair will help mediate disputes and ensure courtesy and balanced air time among all directors. Other times, the chair lacks assertiveness, allowing the most domineering person to railroad through their own agenda—but we'll return to the topic of leadership in the next chapter.

MEETINGS TO BOOK

Once you have read your constitution or memorandum of articles/incorporation documents and offsite strategy reports, and glanced through at least some of the minutes archives, I suggest you sit down with certain division heads to ask any questions you may have. The first three people to talk to are the company secretary, the head of legal, and the director of human resources.

COMPANY SECRETARY

The company secretary will likely be your first point of contact on the board. They likely possess a wealth of institutional knowledge and corporate memory, especially if they've been with the company a long time. They understand board dynamics. They know who gets on with who, and who clashes—and they even know most of the dirt on inappropriate actions (and transactions), even if they'll never tell.

Along with other senior secretaries, the cosec can guide you, explaining which areas are sensitive or resistant to change. Bear in mind that the idea is not to mine this person for information, but to make sure you develop a genuine rapport and trust over time. That way, you're more likely to keep important lines of communication open.

LEGAL

As early as possible, you should speak to the head of your legal department to find out if there are any outstanding lawsuits to be aware of. You need to be thoroughly briefed on any and all major legal issues, legal tussles, DPAs, you name it—whether they're in the past, happening now, or going to happen. For example, there could be cases of disgruntled employees suing for compensation, or vendors claiming they haven't been paid according to contract.

HUMAN RESOURCES

The next staff leader to talk to as soon as possible is the head of human resources. This person should be able to answer any questions you have about the organizational structure of your company. They can also provide cultural insights.

Discussions with HR can help you assess whether the organization is still in line with the constitution or has diverged from its path. They can explain any conspicuous gaps in the organizational chart and they may even gently allude to different points of friction among people. For example, a public company could have an official, written policy to appoint a specific director to defend public interest in various matters—but the company hasn't had a public interest director in months.

Put bluntly, although people are your greatest assets, they're also the source of a lot of problems. Corporate decision-making inevitably involves relationships, culture, and politicking. And, as diversity and inclusion in the boardroom grows, we may well see more friction, at least in the short term.

FOLLOW THE MONEY

The rest of this chapter will focus on how to gather and interpret your company's financials, specifically looking at (internal and external) audits, cost-to-income ratios, and key performance indicators (KPIs), which are benchmarks employees must achieve to earn additional compensation, usually in the form of a bonus.

Why these areas? Because sometimes these financial documents contain major governance red flags, hidden among the columns and rows of figures and sums. I will share some straightforward examples of what to look for, based on my personal experience as either a board member or chair.

AUDITS

There are two company audits to consider, the external audit and the internal audit, and each can reveal helpful information about which areas may warrant further exploration.

External auditors tend to come into the office quarterly or annually to check your books, per IFRS or GAAP regulation. Typically, external auditors just do sampling—not a thorough forensic review—of company books. Because these individuals are trained to quickly identify potential problems, their audit reports are great resources for you when gauging the overall financial health of an organization.

If possible, it's a good idea to speak with external auditors to hear how they interpret the big picture. Did they find any warning signs regarding collection, accounts receivable, costs, etc.? Is the company developing enough succession planning? Whatever the case, external audits can give you a good sense of broad, general issues.

The internal audit is far more depth-driven, thorough, and detailed than the external audit, when it comes to specific areas or processes under review. Depending on the internal auditor's scope, they may be charged with precisely accounting for earnings and expenditures of each division, all the way down to claims for travel expenses.

If nothing else, you'll want to make sure the internal audit regularly assesses every single division. I'll say that again: the internal audit should include information about every single department and team in your organization. Ask to access the company's audit plan to confirm that all departments have been audited within the time span (usually a couple of years) of the audit cycle.

I once served on the board of a company that never audited two of its divisions. After reviewing the organization chart, I noticed these areas simply never appeared in any of the internal audit reports over the course of multiple complete audit cycles. When I asked the internal auditor about this, it was confirmed that senior company management restricted these areas from even basic financial scrutiny.

Later, when someone reportedly found unaccounted-for *literal stacks of cash* on a desk at the company, I was not surprised they were found within one of the two divisions protected from internal audits. Executive management shrugged off the mystery, declaring no further action because security cameras had been (conveniently) out of service, and they didn't deem the amount of money worth investigating.

I dug a bit deeper and found that, within both of these "sacred" unaudited divisions, senior management received nearly double the number of pay raises—in spite of their two-year contracts and higher-than-usual staff attrition rates (always a warning signal).

I've also seen dodgy patterns when it comes to expense claims. Typically, for a lunch or business outing, the most senior manager claims the expense. However, in this case, one group regularly asked a junior team member to claim the expense, after which the same reporting department head would approve it. These expenses went far beyond reasonable travel expenses to include leisure activities, sporting events, luxury rental cars—even an entire island day trip unrelated to business. By strategically distancing company leadership from expense claims, these managers built in plausible deniability around awareness of the costs. After drawing up a flowchart of the expense claims and the approval process within the department, it became clear how they were gaming the system.

Per diem expenses during business trips may seem trivial, but in fact they represent an easy way for people to siphon money away from companies. For example, very senior management may be allocated a driver during trips—however, they decline this service, opting for per diem cash instead. Then, despite receiving per diem cash, they claim parking and mileage expenses in what some refer to as double dipping.

REMUNERATION AND NOMINATION COMMITTEE

One area to pay attention to is the remuneration and nomination committee. Make sure you read the minutes from this group and stay abreast of any patterns when it comes to who gets appointed to leadership positions and who gets bonuses.

For example, those internal audit "no fly zones" I mentioned above? At that same company, a C-level executive requested and received special allocation rights to determine extraordinary bonuses. In the board meeting she explained she intended to give the money to deserving staff who, due to technicalities, hadn't met certain key performance indicators.

As we'll soon see, KPIs can be problematic. Let's say, for example, a company ties KPIs to attendance. If a staff member incurs a serious injury or illness, they may not be eligible for their bonus, through no fault of their own.

I assumed the special bonus allocations were meant to correct misaligned KPIs like this one. Instead, the extra bonuses ended up going—you guessed it—to already overcompensated managers within the two divisions that never got audited.

How did this happen? The simple answer is: the remuneration and nomination committee were not doing their jobs. They allowed a C-level executive to circumvent procedures without so much as a follow-up. They never even asked the executive to provide a list of who received these extra bonuses—a standard procedure that ensures extra bonuses get paid appropriately and documented accordingly.

Even without major red flags like these, you'd be wise to pay close attention to remuneration and nomination committee minutes and reports. If you keep seeing the same people appointed to head multiple committees, for example, you may want to look for signs of nepotism. It's also illuminating just to see the disparity between the highest and lowest full-time earners in an organization.

As a board member, it's your job to analyze salaries. How much do the top four or five earners make? What percentage of company income does this represent? Has everything been audited and approved by remuneration and nomination? Sometimes top executives earn more than 250 times more than junior staff. This kind of top-heavy bloat often highlights major inefficiencies and inequities within the company.

COST-TO-INCOME RATIO

When it comes to efficiency, one particular figure can tell you a lot about a company's finances—namely: cost-to-income ratio. This number measures the cost of running a business compared to its income. The lower the CTI, the more efficient and profitable the company.

When a company's income goes up, management likes to boast about company growth. And while increased revenue is great, it doesn't mean much if the division that earns more immediately and unnecessarily also increases its operating costs. Pay close attention to areas where management brags about revenue increases while their CTI remains exactly the same. This could suggest an ethics issue, or simply unexamined inefficiencies.

Likewise, if income drops while costs remain steady, something needs correcting. Why have sales dipped? Is the company selling a poor product? Have collections faltered? Is it time to rethink market positioning?

A thorough investigation of CTI could reveal, for example, a company's attempt to control costs by not allocating adequate resources to their IT infrastructure, which still depends on systems that use COBOL. While the upgrade is both necessary and long overdue, management may drag their feet to ensure short-term profitability—and a fat remuneration.

You should look at CTI over a long period of time. Whether you're a financial wizard or not, that figure can help alert you to potential issues. After all, even in a household, if your salary increases and you're still living hand to mouth, you should examine whether budgetary indulgences have proportionately increased, alongside your pay raise.

Sometimes remuneration breaks down because the reward system is misguided or opaque. In other words, sometimes key performance indicators (KPIs) incentivize the wrong things. KPIs are benchmarks employees must achieve to earn additional compensation, usually in the form of a bonus. Some KPIs relate to financial targets, and others are non-financial.

Pay attention to whether KPIs are tied to actual revenue results. In some large organizations, a chief strategy officer helps the CEO draft KPIs. If a board nomination and remuneration committee is not permitted to review KPIs, management can create KPIs that disproportionately reward senior staff. For example, division heads may achieve KPIs for simply launching a new product—regardless of its success. I've even seen a KPI tied to how many meetings senior management completes. How difficult is that, right? These are easy ways for high-ranking staff to pad their own KPIs with "bonus targets" that actually fall under the scope of normal employment.

There are other ways non-financial KPIs can be misused. As I mentioned before, I've seen KPIs tied to strict attendance numbers without provisions for extended illness or injury. I've also seen unrealistic scorecards related to public relations metrics, which led departments to overspend in marketing costs or pricey press events—essentially paying for media attention, rather than focusing on running the business in a way that drives organic, earned coverage.

Perhaps the greatest real danger with KPIs has to do with sales. I once met an interesting military salesperson who sold equipment around the world. His company set sky-high sales KPIs, and he soon became the top performer—until he was caught by the FBI for bribing people in Southeast Asia. According to him, his company pushed him so hard that eventually bribery became the only reliable way he could meet his KPIs.

Every time I hear something like this, it makes me wonder: Did the board of that company know and allow this company culture to continue? To what extent had they really analyzed the system of incentives and rewards among their sales staff? Often, when numbers look good, scrutiny decreases. After all, people figure, why question a "good" thing?

As you may have gathered by now, the sad truth is that too many board directors fail to even regularly skim—let alone thoroughly read—their agendas, board papers, and minutes. This is especially true for career directors who sit on multiple boards simply to maintain status and collect fees. Often these professional directors don't even stay for the entire meeting, instead rushing off to clock in at yet another board meeting, which entitles them to collect more attendance fees. People like that aren't likely to look too closely at one individual consistently hitting suspiciously high sales numbers in Southeast Asia.

DON'T COMPROMISE, ANALYZE

When you finally walk through those imposing boardroom doors, you're likely eager to contribute. Maybe you've educated yourself about ESG sustainability, and you have big ideas to share—and that's wonderful. I hope you never lose that foundational empathy or sense of radical accountability to all stakeholders.

But please, take your time and proceed with caution.

Again, if you come in guns blazing, ready to reform the world, you may find yourself cut off from off-record information flow. Perhaps you'll even end up on the receiving end of constant interruptions and derisive or even belligerent remarks. If this sounds a bit like a petty high school cafeteria drama, well, that image may not be too far off (take it from someone with decades of international boardroom experience).

Your first job is simply to gather information. Listen to the CEO and other C-suite leaders to understand their roles and responsibilities and find out what they're concerned about and where they need help. Watch how people comport themselves, interact with others, and respond to meeting dynamics. Confer with your cosec, legal team, and HR rep for answers and insights. Finally, read between the lines of minutes, internal audits, and other key documents to help understand company history and identify key goals, issues, and patterns—including potential red flags.

This kind of ongoing, critical board assessment is what governance sustainability is all about. Don't forget that politics is often so much rhetoric and campaigning. Even honest management curates the truth for board consumption; after all, the board determines their bonuses. Good board members do their homework, listen carefully, interpret figures, and cross-reference documents to spot disparities between what people say and what's really going on. This is what stakeholders want and need in board members.

Perhaps above all, the board chair sets the tone and parameters of behavior and practices that are tolerated within the boardroom walls. The next chapter will focus on understanding board leadership, from the chair and C-team to board committee chairs.

We'll explore power plays, committee functions, and overall how board leadership impacts politics and culture, either promoting or impeding sustainable growth.

CHAPTER 8

LEADERSHIP AND POWER DYNAMICS

Anyone who's spent any amount of time in a corporate setting has dealt with power struggles and toxic leadership. Once you've ascended to the boardroom, you can safely expect more of the same—only magnified.

This chapter on leadership and power dynamics will examine how both board leaders and company executives influence culture by setting the tone from the top—for better or worse. We'll explore patterns that groom or reinforce notions of inequality, as well as common political tactics that either promote or impede good decision-making. Throughout, I will offer tips on how to anticipate and address those, especially if you find yourself chairing a committee—or even the entire board—yourself.

"KNOW YOUR PLACE"

Even something as benign as a corporate event can reveal patterns of toxic management. I once sat on a board for a Malaysian company that organized an all-company party, ostensibly to allow staff to engage with senior management and get to know new board leadership.

In our part of the world, we enjoy a wide range of native tropical fruits, including one particular variety, called the durian, lauded as "the king of fruit." It's widely considered an acquired taste, due to its rather putrid scent. However, considering the exorbitant price of top-quality durians—the fruits have sold in Thai auctions for tens of thousands of US dollars—it's a taste that mainly the privileged and elite have the luxury to acquire.

While I'm admittedly not a fan myself, many people adore this fruit. So plenty of staff members were looking forward to the first-rate fruit spreads management advertised for the party.

In the end, however, senior management segregated its fruit service into two parts. They set out one table reserved only for C-suite managers and board directors, which they adorned with the coveted durian and other luxury fruits.

Everyone else was restricted to the second-rate (cheap) fruit table.

This is comparable to setting out a fine Petrus Bordeaux for senior staff and serving everyone else bottom-shelf plonk wine. Furthermore, this organization so closely chaperones its top-level leaders that most of them enjoyed their expensive fruit blissfully unaware of the fact that regular staff were cordoned off from that particular room by security.

While it hardly qualifies as some major governance abuse, to many at the company, this ungracious stunt epitomized the company's ongoing patterns of inequality and disrespect by senior management toward more junior colleagues. It prompted one young woman, who had been with the company for years, to finally resign. For her, this display confirmed that, despite new board management, the rot of unchecked elitism ran so deep within senior management that she no longer wished to trade her time or talent for such treatment.

BOARD AND COMMITTEE LEADERSHIP

The first time I ever chaired a board meeting, the cosec offered to carry my bags. After I politely declined, I was dismayed (but not surprised) to learn that I was the first chair of this board to ever insist on carrying my own bags. Small acts like this can help nurture a culture of respect and accountability, rather than one of dominance.

Sadly, I have seen brash, entitled directors arrive at a hotel, announce themselves as a board member of the group that owns the hotel, then rudely admonish the bellhop who stumbled while carrying their bags, or the valet who didn't give their car priority.

Unfortunately, such personalities often rise to positions of power, and board leaders can only do so much to keep bad behavior in check. That said, the chair of the board largely sets the tone for tolerated behavior—at least, around the boardroom table itself. As a board chair myself, I've had many occasions to address ingrained, dysfunctional habits by directors.

You may recall the story from Chapter 2 about the noisy espresso machine. Some directors employ distraction tactics like this to assert some sense of authority, or possibly just to amuse themselves. Don't be surprised if, for example, directors request snacks like potato crisps, only to noisily, shamelessly crunch their food into live microphones while other members try to speak.

Certain very aggressive directors on one board would regularly interrupt a particular fellow director with a meticulous, halting style of speech. In my very first meeting I had to insist: "Please, could you let her finish?" It only took a few firm reminders to stop this behavior.

As a board leader, it's important to me to cultivate discussion that encourages everybody to speak up—and disagree, when needed, even with the board chair or CEO. How can a company succeed and compete internationally if its board members refuse to listen or try to conceal problems within the organization?

Finally, to combat and prevent corruption, board leaders should nurture a culture of integrity. As a board leader, I do not mind having the reputation of being a stickler for the rules. In my mind, board members can never be "too forthright."

Never forget that discussions in the boardroom will determine whether the company and its shareholders do well. Despite popular misconception by certain directors, sitting on a board is not just about door prizes, fancy titles, and "first" or business class flights.

DEVILS IN THE DETAILS

The sad truth is that too many directors consider board appointments as payouts. For example, when directors get paid per meeting, some board members will try to arrange extra board meetings, typically through playing politics with senior management. Normally, matters related to board fees must be approved by shareholders, but some board directors will try to leverage perceived problems to convene meetings outside of "business as usual," just to squeeze a bit more out of the company.

If you know what to look for as board or committee chair, you can quickly identify and correct procedural patterns, within and outside of meetings, intended to either exploit company resources or circumvent thorough discussion—whether by fellow board members or management. This section identifies how to approach meeting agendas and minutes, and certain key policies, to promote greater transparency and accountability within the boardroom.

DCRS

Chapter 6 began with a story about a directors' circular resolution (DCR) a board once tried to pass through for approval late on Friday evening—despite high stakes (a transaction representing hundreds of millions) and key errors (incorrect bank information).

I bring this up again because it's worth underscoring how DCRs can be misused. Namely, as a new director, you should make sure your company's DCRs require unanimous board approval—not just majority approval—to pass decisions outside of convened meetings. Otherwise, some board members may attempt to bypass directors less amenable to the resolution.

When majority rule is sufficient to pass a DCR, resolutions on contentious issues can be approved without proper discussion or transparency—indeed, without all directors even being informed of the process.

I can recall, for example, the CEO of one company proposing a restructuring plan. When some board members requested more information, the CEO pushed for a decision by majority DCR, collaborated with the board chair to cherry pick which directors would sign, then slipped the restructuring plan through without even notifying the remaining board members.

This is one surefire way for boards to devolve into infighting. If your company's DCR policy is majority only, propose it be changed straightaway to unanimous approval. Healthy, transparent companies require unanimous DCRs, then—as a reminder and paper trail—they list all DCRs signed since the last board meeting on the front page of the agenda paper. This helps regulators monitor companies and ensure against irregularities. Even if you are not a board or committee chair, you can introduce such a proposal. Otherwise, you very well may find yourself or others excluded from vital decision-making processes.

AGENDAS

As you review meeting agendas, the first area to look at is the timing allocated for each item. I always find it amusing when a routine item intended for notation gets allocated the same amount of time as urgent, complex topics, such as an auditing issue, financial proposal, or organizational change. When this occurs, it may indicate that, for whatever reason, management does not want the major issues to be discussed thoroughly.

If you are the chair of the board or of a committee, you must make sure that you set enough time for topics and allow opportunities for breakout group discussion. Management may try to push for an even ten minutes for each topic. However, in reality, certain discussions often exceed the allotted time, so try to anticipate the actual time needed for each item, based on the relative complexity, urgency, and level of controversy for each.

Far too often, directors cannot stay for the entire meeting. As chair, I also try to find out in advance which board members or committee members will leave early. That way, if we have important external presentations, I can schedule those first on the agenda. If the presentation is particularly contentious, I sometimes won't even include them in the agenda for that meeting. Instead, I'll suggest a special discussion on this topic to ensure all directors firmly understand the issues at stake (and make sure it appears later in the meeting minutes). Otherwise some people may deliberately come late so they can claim ignorance of the issue, stating, "I didn't attend the briefing."

I remember once asking a colleague how he would deal with some challenging agenda issues, and he replied, "Don't worry; I've timed it so I'll get phone calls and I'll step out."

When this occurs, the minutes will show that so-and-so was not included in that discussion, because they left the room. Then, if there's a liability problem, that individual cannot be implicated. You'll soon notice that many senior board members who sit on multiple boards rarely stay for entire meetings.

LIVE SECTION

In the last chapter, I talked about something in meeting minutes called "matters arising," which require management to follow up and update the board at the next meeting.

If the matters arising happen to be something that management would rather avoid, they may dodge the issue during the next meeting, claiming they didn't have time to get around to this and promising a later update. After a few such evasive maneuvers, issues easily get lost in the shuffle.

As a board chair, I address this by keeping a list of unresolved matters in what I call the "live section" of each meeting "minutes" and have it listed in the agenda. Relevant directors and executives must give an update on each outstanding live section item at every meeting. These updates get added to the live section until we can close the item, either because we're satisfied the matter has found resolution, or because it's no longer relevant. Sometimes people grumble, asking if we can shelve certain topics until a set date when things can progress. However, I find that a diligent live section check-in for matters arising holds management accountable—especially to important matters such as an upcoming lawsuit or M&A.

In effect, the live section creates an audit trail of delays and obstacles faced when resolving sticky issues. In some cases, it also catalogs deliberate inaction by certain parties. Other times, live matters arising can help management avoid careless oversight related to tedious but important processes. For example, if you're dealing with another jurisdiction and a document has to be submitted to a court overseas, you absolutely cannot miss the filing deadline for that document submission.

BOARD APPROVALS

Sometimes senior management attempts to push board approval on certain matters through improper channels, often in collusion with key board directors. For example, a senior executive may ask a subcommittee to illicitly approve a proposal subject to full board consideration.

I once sat on a board where the CFO tried to push through a multimillion-dollar project to create a pool of money to invest in companies exploring different available fintech technologies. When the board voted not to approve the idea, she went to a subcommittee chair the night before a company holiday, claimed she already had approval from the previous board, and asked the subcommittee chair to sign off on the plan. Because the project failed to define clear objectives or limitations on who approved these investments or how, it devolved into a slush fund she used to invest into any company that fit her fancy.

Now, if ever it happens that the previous board approved a project that never got executed, always review the matter and put it to a new vote. It may be that the project was never realized because it's a contentious issue or faulty plan. Perhaps this project does not align with the current business strategy, mission, or values.

COMMITTEES

Earlier in my career, I often sat on boards with only two committees: the audit committee and the remuneration and nomination committee. That was it. Now you also see committees for risk assessment, and increasingly, for both sustainability and technology.

Within the next, final chapter, we'll delve into what makes a good sustainability committee, as well as how committees can effectively engage with stakeholders. For now, let's briefly discuss the traditional "core" committees of audit, and remuneration and nomination.

AUDIT COMMITTEES

If you are chairing the board, or you've been appointed to the audit committee, it's a good idea to study the culture and history of your organization's finances. Schedule a conversation with external auditors to find out how audit issues have been handled in the past. Check for any changes in the authority manual. Perhaps most importantly, examine the cost-to-income ratio across the board and compare CTIs among specific divisions to see how costs are managed versus revenue growth. This is a quick-and-dirty ratio that can tell you a lot about the company very quickly.

When analyzing your CTI, you'll want to specifically look at capital expenditure (capex) and resource allocation. If you ask the right questions to internal and external auditors, you can quickly determine whether costs are under control and resources properly allocated. For example, has there been a tendency to allocate more resources to weaker areas, and if so, is that money being properly used to remedy the situation—or has it served to essentially reward underperforming staff?

Sometimes, expense claims are not properly approved. Perhaps you have a CFO who habitually approves dubious per diem expenses without questioning a thing. Sometimes companies claim that the CEO should sign off on the chairperson's expenses; however, this shouldn't be the case. Technically, the CEO ranks junior to the board chair. As such, the board chair should approve claims by the CEO, and a senior independent director should approve claims by the board chair. This may seem obvious, but as I mentioned in the last chapter, I have seen CEOs and other C-level executives ask junior staff to expense items so they can sign off and approve the claims—mainly exorbitant leisure activities on the company's dime.

Keep a close eye on business travel expenses, particularly if senior management claims to need private jets "for security" or other reasons. I once met with an executive who took the company's private jet on a detour from Europe to North America and back to fetch their favorite ski instructor for an Alpine retreat—as a company expense.

Before moving on, I'd like to address one last point. I have heard some people talk about expanding the audit committee to include risk assessment, or even merge separate audit and risk committees into one.

This is *not* recommended.

Put simply, audits look to the past, while risk assessment looks to the future. These are two very different functions, and while they certainly should work in communication and collaboration with each other, it's not realistic to expect the same individuals to fulfill both roles. Internal and external audits can get extremely detailed and time-intensive. Merging risk with audit would require unreasonable time commitments for these committee members. Such a hybrid would compromise risk assessment, given the amount of time and effort inevitably consumed by audit issues.

For those directors appointed to the remuneration and nomination committee, you should take at least a day to read the past committee decisions and the committee terms of reference. The same goes for the chair of the board.

By thoroughly understanding past meeting notes and reports, you should be able to discern decision-making trends and policies. Have KPIs been set up to reward sustainable growth, or are they incentivizing arbitrary or even counterproductive metrics? You may find that KPIs for senior management are much easier to achieve than those of more junior staff.

Remuneration and nomination are often lumped under one committee, but increasingly companies are splitting these into two—and for good reason. When the same people are responsible for interviewing and selecting company leaders and also determining their salaries, these individuals become extremely powerful. Yes, these decisions typically require full board approval, but not until significant legwork and tentative negotiations have taken place. As such, the board feels pressure to approve hiring and remuneration decisions.

Carefully examine your company's organizational chart looking for any major gaps. You may notice positions remaining unfilled for extended periods of time. If so, have those same division heads requested more or steeper raises than others? Some management leaves intentional gaps in their teams so they can request more compensation for themselves.

The same goes for divisions with higher-than-average attrition rates. High turnover is a very strong indicator of toxic management. Similarly, ineffective department heads often sacrifice junior staff who call them out or whose talent and competency threaten to "outshine" them, leading to a revolving door department staff.

Companies with these kinds of problems often end up "top heavy," with an excess of leadership positions or staggering pay gaps between senior and junior staff. If you notice conspicuous disparities, look more closely at those empty positions and pay metrics. Review past exit interviews for potential problem areas (major red flag if there aren't any exit interviews). Are certain executives given undue power over hires and salaries? Are selection committees doing their due diligence to pull in a sufficient pool of qualified candidates, or do they unofficially pre-approve a known recruit, then conduct one or two brief, perfunctory interviews?

MEETING MINUTES REDUX

Now that we've reviewed basic committee structures, let's return to the matter of meeting minutes. In particular, we'll talk about how to help ensure transparency in meeting minutes, the importance of reviewing and confirming minutes, and how to keep "matters arising" from falling through the cracks.

"PLEASE MINUTE THIS"

Remember this phrase and use it during board meetings whenever you'd like certain comments recorded verbatim in the meeting minutes. Any board member can ask the cosec to minute something.

Otherwise, meeting minutes can get rather vague: "The board

had a discussion on X and it was resolved Y." Nothing about precisely who said what. If you're on a board with a lot of lawsuits, or where individuals haven't followed proper due process—they didn't get the right regulatory approvals, for example—detailed meeting minutes become very important.

In some cases, management or board leaders discreetly ask the cosec to leave out certain things. I have attended board meetings rife with major lawsuits and dirty deals, which the minutes somehow failed to mention. You can avoid this by getting on the record asking the cosec to minute important or sensitive information.

When it comes to matters of ESG sustainability, minutes are key. If a corporate board considers a deforestation proposal to build new mines, for example, ask about how the company assesses environmental impact, and make sure the cosec minutes the discussion. If that topic doesn't turn up in the minutes, request a playback of the meeting recording with the cosec.

Alternatively, let's say there's a debate about foreign labor costs, and your CEO insists on ignoring poor working conditions. His dismissive comments likely will go unrecorded unless you or another board member says, "I have a different view on that," and asks the cosec to minute the exchange. Even if the CEO wants the discussion struck from the minutes, you have the right to stand your ground and insist. Otherwise, certain individuals will try to shape the conversation and decision-making with no accountability for what they have said.

Obviously, don't overdo it, or you may end up with a hundred pages of minutes no one reads. That's not good for transparency either. Instead, review the agenda for important issues and draft your comments in advance of meetings. Sometimes I print mine out and provide a copy to the cosec to minute verbatim. This is especially advisable if something is going to trial and/or you suspect misbehavior among board or executive leaders.

REVIEW AND CONFIRM MINUTES

If you serve as chair of the board, you personally must ensure that meeting minutes have been accurately, transparently recorded with no doctoring. As soon as possible after each meeting, carefully review the draft minutes before confirming them with a signature.

Meeting minutes must be confirmed in a timely manner to ensure the proper execution of decisions. I've been in meetings where directors make a contentious decision, then, when execution fails, disgruntled board members have the excuse that the minutes were never confirmed.

Sometimes delays can be expected, especially when meeting minutes go on for fifty pages or more. In these situations, the board chair can ask the cosec to type up an extract of key discussion points for priority confirmation. This can circulate via email for board confirmation before the executive team executes—and this way nobody can cop out.

OFF-RECORD DISCUSSIONS

After a board meeting has been officially adjourned with the words, "meeting closed," no other comments or discussions can be minuted. Sometimes this is helpful for casual discussion, information gathering, or even unofficial votes related to new matters.

That said, proceed cautiously when it comes to "off the record" discussions. On one board, I recall a particularly sensitive issue with liability implications. External lawyers had explained the actions needed to avoid a lawsuit. After the meeting was closed, off the record, the chair informally discussed our options and we held an unofficial vote.

When the minutes circulated, this vote of course had not been recorded. One particular board member, who was trying to curry favor with the regulating body, called up the cosec—at midnight—when he saw the first draft and screamed at her to change the minutes to include the vote. Despite this harassment, the cosec reviewed the meeting tapes and clearly heard the words "meeting over." As such, she had to respect that the subsequent vote had indeed been off the record.

It's customary to have such director-only sessions following board meetings. Typically, after the executives leave, directors linger for informal conversations or unofficial votes or views. While these can be hugely helpful, it's still wise to be mindful of what you say—and always assume there's a chance that these "off the record" discussions may nevertheless escape the room.

DIGITAL COMMUNICATIONS

Speaking of "off record," be mindful of how you engage in digital board communications—for example, group chats on messaging apps like WhatsApp—especially when you serve as a board or committee chair.

Often the cosec uses these apps to alert board members when a system goes down, or there's been a change in meeting schedule.

Sometimes they send updates about developing situations, for example a breach in data security. While the immediacy of this communication method is helpful, bear in mind that you may not be able to retain a record of past discussions. Always print or otherwise back up sensitive communications like this.

Some board members refuse to join communications apps and group chats due to privacy concerns about forwarding messages or accidentally sharing texts with the wrong people. Be very cautious about commenting on group chats. While most board members respect the confidentiality of board communications, others quite enjoy cloak-and-dagger power plays. You do not want to see a careless comment shared with the wrong shareholder, executive, or even media outlet.

CULTURE OF MANAGEMENT

While the board chair can influence corporate culture and politics, directors also must navigate, and sometimes contend with, the tone set by the CEO and other C-level leaders.

I recommend inviting more junior management to board meetings whenever appropriate. Observing how different levels of management interact can be quite illuminating. Pay attention, for example, to who can best answer the questions posed by the board. Is it the CEO, senior exec, or C-level minus two? You can quickly assess which person has the most knowledge about an issue, how well they communicate with one another, and what kind of succession planning makes sense.

Sometimes in response to highly technical questions, management hesitates or even declines to answer, declaring the matter "too high level" for the board to appreciate. To me, this implies the board is considered too simple or ignorant to understand the issues. It's also a convenient save when the person presenting doesn't quite know the full answer.

When boardroom issues become highly technical or contentious, requesting and previewing a summary report of such matters before the meeting, complete with definitions, metrics, and resources, can provide insight that supports a productive discussion.

Circulate this summary report among the board and encourage directors—particularly those with relevant expertise—to submit questions in advance. Build in time for specific breakout groups to deal with highly technical questions, and make sure you learn exactly what is at stake. What are the risks? What resources are needed? After all, most of what happens in a boardroom is about people, money, and strategy.

At the end of the day, there's only so much you can do with exceptionally dysfunctional executives. Remember the CEO I mentioned who changed the authority manual so that he could personally hire every employee? So insistent was this man on absolute loyalty that he created a separate department designed to temporarily or permanently exile staff who dared question or defy him (unofficially referred to as "Siberia" or the "shaming department").

While this is a rather extreme example, it well illustrates one central point: board leadership is not a life of glamor. It is an ongoing process of firefighting—all the while steering a company toward savvy, sustainable growth.

There is a lot to unpack when it comes to how boardroom leadership impacts the culture and politics of both company management and shareholder relations. However, responsible board leadership extends far beyond C-suite, and even investor, relations.

I believe the single most important aspect of corporate stewardship has more to do with how well the board interacts with everyone—from junior staff to NGOs to communities impacted by business, both locally and globally. The next chapter will dive deeper into the importance of open dialogue with all stakeholders—especially when things go wrong.

CHAPTER 9

STAKEHOLDER ENGAGEMENT

We all understand the power of the shareholders' voice. After all, they're the ones who vote directors into the boardroom. When they're not keen on the direction of a company, activist shareholders sometimes use this voice to rally for change.

In 2021, a small hedge fund called Engine No. 1 released a white paper suggesting a strategy for ExxonMobil to remain relevant in a world transitioning from fossil fuels. Their message wasn't about abruptly stripping assets or eliminating jobs, but rather about allocating more resources to sustainable energy initiatives.

Engine No. 1 only held 0.02 percent of Exxon's shares, but their 82-page proposal to "re-energize Exxon" aimed to educate the company's three largest shareholders, Vanguard, BlackRock, and State Street. Especially since those investment companies' publicly stated goals included steeply reducing their portfolios' carbon emissions.

This kind of shareholder activism tends to make waves. NGOs

will sometimes buy the minimum number of shares required to attend a company's annual general meeting (AGM)—only to show up and protest environmental or social abuses. In one particularly memorable AGM, I watched demonstrators march in carrying stuffed animals covered in ketchup, symbols of the company's destruction of wildlife habitats.

These stories underscore the importance of stakeholder engagement—not only your company's largest shareholders, but also the full range of investors, as well as your company's entire staff, consumers, business partners, and the communities and ecosystems its operations serve and impact.

I've been on the investment side for long enough to know that many company leaders are simply not receptive. Too many never bother to examine stakeholder issues, or even find out what they are.

There are a lot of different stakeholders to engage. In terms of capital markets alone, you have so many participants: stockbrokers, fund managers, retail investors, pension funds, and mutual funds—to name a few. Each kind of investor has different needs and perspectives.

Of course, you cannot follow the advice of every single stakeholder, but you can listen. And you will be a far more effective board member when you understand the full range of stakeholder interests and concerns.

This includes the people who form the organization itself—from C-suite to entry level—and NGOs and other communities impacted by your business. This chapter will explore these different stakeholders and offer strategies for engaging with each—from addressing whistleblowers, to setting up advisory boards, to navigating NGOs and annual general meetings with shareholders.

Because this book deals centrally with matters of ESG sustainability, this chapter will also examine the importance of a sustainability committee and chief sustainability officer when it comes to stakeholder engagement.

Let's start with the shareholders, including both institutional (focusing mainly on the ESG impact of global pension funds) and retail investors.

PENSION FUNDS AND INSTITUTIONAL INVESTORS

Global pension funds were among the first signatories to join the United Nations Principles of Responsible Investing. Among institutional investors, pension funds still seem to lead the charge for ESG sustainability.

The sustainability focus of pension funds largely reflects highly engaged, conscientious individual investors: the pension fund contributors themselves. For example, teachers generally do not want their pensions invested in companies profiting from child labor or flagrantly polluting oceans.

When workers contribute to state pension funds, they receive regular statements listing all the companies involved in the fund. If they see something they don't like, they can speak up about it. If there are enough individual investors who agree, they can all make an impact by speaking up together.

Many state pensions have already divested from tobacco companies, following decades of research about the dangers of both smoking and secondhand smoke. These funds are poised for a similar exit from fossil fuels. Some major New York pension funds have already divested from fossil fuels, and other states are considering the same.

Of course, many people still don't give a toss about anything but their dividends. However, that seems to be shifting rapidly, especially when it comes to climate change. The consequences of a rapidly heating planet are beginning to change coastlines, agricultural patterns, insurance costs, stranded assets, and more.

Pension fund trustees tend to listen to their stakeholders—or risk protests and bad publicity. Sometimes they also farm money out to external asset managers—whether listed, private equity venture, or real estate—and when they do, they often pass along other strict ESG requirements, helping to spread sustainable practices across the market.

RETAIL INVESTORS

Many retail investors are quite ESG conscious—and this trend is growing rapidly. However, among private equity investors, too many view sustainability as some nuisance that threatens to cut into profits. They're not especially concerned about climate change or plastics or data mismanagement. They just want easy private equity financing, and they keep their companies unlisted to avoid abiding by listing rules.

Those retail investors who define success only by money often respond only to material consequences. This is where enforceability and standardization can really help. If conscience doesn't get their attention, fines and lawsuits might.

That said, a growing number of private equity investors require that private equity firms build ESG framework metrics and timelines into their investee companies—similar to pension asset owners and external pension fund managers, who typically want to know that the companies they invest in pay attention to ESG standards.

ANNUAL GENERAL MEETINGS

The annual general meeting (AGM) is the one time each year when all investors—from pension funds to retail investors to activist shareholders—can engage directly with a company's board and gather information. It's vital to show you're listening to shareholders, not just showering them with door gifts and meal vouchers.

Be warned, however, that AGMs can get chaotic. Emotions can run high (especially when you review staff remunerations and investors see how much executives get paid). Some shareholders seem to look for excuses to act out. I once chaired an AGM where a shareholder began ranting, raving, and even cursing because he didn't get a printed copy of the annual report—all in front of thousands of people. In response, I stood up and said firmly, "I'm happy to have all your views, but please mind your language. This is a general meeting." I then walked down to the corner of the stage, handed my copy to the secretary, and asked her to pass it on to the man.

Because I have worked as a fund manager for so long, I also appreciate the experience of being a shareholder at an annual general meeting. For this reason, I err on the side of over-emphasizing open dialogue at AGMs. As board chair, I constantly open the floor for questions when we meet with shareholders—so much so that I heard snide remarks from one director: "When is she going to stop asking for more questions from the floor?"

When we had a free moment, I turned to this director and quietly explained, "This is the only time in a year that shareholders meet the board officially. Big investors, small—it doesn't matter. We need to give them their time."

STAFF ENGAGEMENT

Your company staff may not be the ones making noise at your AGMs, but, as the ones who design, manufacture, sell, and distribute your products they arguably represent your company's most important stakeholders.

Too many corporations view human resources as merely that—replaceable resources to mine, manage, and exploit. However, the 2020 coronavirus pandemic has dramatically changed the way people view and talk about their work. Global shutdowns have demonstrated the viability of remote work. In 2021, more than 47 million workers in America voluntarily quit their jobs in what was dubbed the Great Resignation.

As I write this, countries like the UK, Australia, and France have reported similar upticks in employee resignations, and workers around the world report unprecedented dissatisfaction and interest in exploring new career options.

So how can corporate boards better serve employees? Once again, the matter boils down to culture, transparency, and communication. Board leaders should find opportunities to open lines of communication at every level of the organization, from a sensible whistleblowing policy to better engagement with upper management.

For example, one chairman I know in Singapore regularly attends management committee meetings. Granted, the committee will send a summary to the board, but he also learns a lot simply by observing discussions and due diligence—and management welcomes his attendance.

However, when company politics get toxic, you may see a staunch resistance to engagement with management and company staff outside of regularly scheduled board meetings. When I became chair at one organization, the previous chairman warned me that the one and only time he decided to pop into a management committee meeting, he was accused of breaching his non-executive role by chairing the meeting—even though he'd only quietly observed.

On hearing that, I hardly dared to leave my floor. In fact, I only ventured down the stairs a couple of times during my tenure as board chair. One marked a visit to internal audit and IT, after hearing a tip that these departments tended to stay very late, without adequate areas to rest and sleep.

Major IT problems or audit deadlines can keep such staff in the office until 4 or 5 a.m., alternately working and resting at their desks—often getting neck aches for their trouble. After asking around, we found a department willing to immediately send over extra bean bag chairs—which truly made all the difference. Sometimes the simplest things can vastly improve a work environment.

My second trip down the stairs was to send off a staff member who had served the company for more than thirty-five years. I wrote a letter of thank you, which I hand-delivered to her. When she told me she had never met any of the chairs before, I was surprised and dismayed.

In response, I initiated a monthly 11 o'clock Tea with the Board Chair for staff members to meet with me in an informal capacity. Whenever staff members came in, I would begin by saying, "We know you're not here to complain about your boss. I just wanted to say thank you." Meanwhile, I knew they had ways to communicate with me if something needed to be reported to the board—and indeed, I began receiving more direct notes and tips about staff concerns following this gesture.

Perhaps unsurprisingly, this tea caused a bit of a ruckus. Management wasn't keen on unsupervised engagement between staff and board leaders, so they tried to curate who could participate. However, I stood my ground and insisted on an open door policy for all.

I believe you can't understand what's truly going on in a company unless you interact with staff all the way to the junior level. Not listening to or engaging with people does not make their concerns go away; it rather serves to inflame issues. Meanwhile, social work gestures like these promote mutual trust and respect among ranks.

Many directors and executives hold onto the erroneous view that a corporate leader must remain ever tough, restrained, and distant. I disagree. Yes, there's a time and place for being tough. But there's also a time and place to relax a bit, show your human side, and actually connect with people. This may have to do with how I was raised to treat everybody with the same level of respect. My mother didn't hesitate to keep VIPs waiting while she treated sick children, regardless of their status or their family's ability to pay.

I've found that morale particularly benefits from things like sports days and family picnics. As a board director, make it a priority to show up to these functions—oh, and by the way, don't forget to actually have fun! When I served as board chair at one company, they organized a company-wide foot race. So I decided to join—much to the staff's surprise and management's dismay.

"You're going to run?" asked senior management.

"Sure," I said. "Why not?" I may not have won the race, but it was so fun and relaxed.

I remember one executive team asking how I could care so much about individuals, but remain so tough on matters of governance reform. These things are not mutually exclusive, but rather deeply interconnected and even symbiotic. Simply listening to staff can go a long way in improving performance. However, poor governance practices—such as revising authority limits to gain absolute control over staff hires, or gaming the system to increase executive perks—do nothing but foment dissatisfaction and dissent.

I am a firm believer in open door policies and genuine staff engagement. Running a foot race, saying thank you, asking how people are doing and fully listening to the answer over tea—none of this has to mean letting your guard down or letting people walk all over you. In my experience, such gestures instead strengthen trust and respect, and help build morale.

I developed this approach early in my career, while working for AIG. I found that the culture in that organization prioritized transparency and open communication. Management was always asking, "How can we get better?"

More importantly, they welcomed responses from everyone—in particular, from those with subject matter expertise, whether from the C-suite or an administrator. I believe that if someone—anyone—knows the answer or could shed light on a problem, invite them in to talk about it. Why wait another month to filter the discussion through the organization via secondhand and thirdhand memos?

Given this transparency and open communication at AIG, when I was there, I had no qualms about sharing concerns with my senior bosses—about the organization, about the markets, anything at all. In our presentations, we were encouraged to report on what went right, but also: What went wrong? And what are we doing to improve? This atmosphere encourages honest self-reflection and learning from—rather than covering up—mistakes.

TRANSPARENCY IN MANAGEMENT

Speaking of covering up, sometimes companies try to hide information under the guise of transparency. For example, rather than calling the board's attention to certain hot-button issues, they might bury these in an enormous stack of meeting notes with no appendix, no table of contents, and no executive summary—all delivered twenty-four hours before a board meeting. This way, they discourage busy board members from actually reading their reports, while retaining the ability to say, "We gave you notes on that; they were clearly defined on page 465."

If you are chairing a board committee, always prepare a thorough summary of key issues discussed, recommended, and decided, to go along with the meeting minutes. This summary should be less than five pages long.

I also recommend you reference the authority manual and terms of reference to help gauge the transparency of your organization. Board directors should have access to exit interviews and manager reviews, for example.

Invite managers below the C-suite to the boardroom. Get a sense of where the problems are. Executives at the top tend to be pretty guarded compared to more junior staff. Middle management is often more willing to discuss what's really going on versus those at the top, who may be more worried about their cushy KPIs.

Encourage everyone to speak—and even to disagree with your view. Support voting on issues. There is nothing wrong with considering other points of view. Asking for the opinion of junior staff doesn't make you a weak leader, nor does it obligate you to follow anyone else's advice. However, it does make you a more informed decision-maker.

WHISTLEBLOWERS

Upon joining the board of one company, I asked how many staff or community whistleblowing complaints they receive each year, and they proudly said, "None!"

That's when I replied, "There's clearly something wrong with your whistleblower policy then. Who is in charge of receiving these?" No one on the board knew. Clearly, this board was not in the practice of encouraging management, staff, or community members to speak up.

Always make sure you understand a company's whistleblowing policy. Find out precisely whether a company dictates official channels for whistleblowing complaints and who exactly receives and responds to such tips. Often, internal audit teams review the whistleblowing tips. Other boards have these directed to the chair or to a senior independent director.

In many cultures, people hesitate or even refuse to use such official channels for fear of exposure and reprisal. I believe that, to protect anonymity, whistleblowing should be allowed in any form or format. It can be an unsigned document slipped under your door, or through a comment box unmonitored by CCTV cameras. Ideally, staff should know one or two trusted board members they can directly or indirectly reach out to.

When people understand there's a real possibility for things to improve—when they know senior management or board leaders will not tolerate corruption—they speak up. However, the minute they suspect the culture at the top condones poor behavior, the whistleblowing tends to slow or even stop. People understand that nothing will be done, plus they don't want to risk punishment or losing their job.

Not long after I spoke up to this board about whistleblowing, I began receiving anonymous "love letters" outlining issues within the organization. On yet another board, staff members found out where I lived and sent brown envelopes full of documents and photos, showing, for example, that when management hired a company to do office renovations, the same company was spotted doing renovations on the CEO's house—which later turned out to be charged as a company expense.

If the whistleblowing complaint seems legitimate and serious enough, the board should recommend investigating the issue through a direct inquiry. If the complaint involves a lower-ranking officer, assess whether the CEO or the C-suite team may be implicated. If not, senior management may investigate and report back to the board.

However, if there's any concern about the involvement of executive management, the board should set up a task force to complete a direct inquiry into the complaint. Generally, this involves a couple independent directors, as well as the internal audit department. The task force reviews relevant documents and interviews people who may be involved in the alleged wrongdoing or who may be able to provide information.

If the task force cannot find sufficient basis for the complaint, they may drop it. Otherwise, it's time for consequence management. For sticky issues, legal counsel may advise on how to either sanction or sever ties with problematic individuals.

If you discourage transparency within the organization, whistleblowers may skip the board and report issues directly to regulatory organizations or government authorities, such as the US Department of Justice, the UK Serious Fraud Office, or France's National Financial Prosecutor's Office. Next thing you know, you have an officer dispatched to your organization to monitor graft, not to mention a media blowup.

Quite often whistleblowers will create an anonymous blog or

Twitter account that exposes allegations against a company. Once they release details and data—or threaten to—people tend to sit up and notice.

I personally prefer to learn about company issues in the boardroom rather than reading about them in a newspaper or on social media platforms. We should be big enough to confront people and issues head on, rather than letting uncomfortable topics snowball into major legal forays and PR nightmares.

PUBLIC ENGAGEMENT

The process for receiving and responding to complaints should not be limited to internal whistleblowing, but also extend to external stakeholders. Whether through critical white papers or performative AGM demonstrations, individuals, NGOs, and other groups sometimes resort to highly public means when corporations fail to listen to or proactively engage with them.

Whether they are official shareholders or not, such individuals and organizations should be regarded by ESG-minded board members as valuable resources and allies. Many NGOs, for example, advocate for ecological interests, amplify community voices, and can help corporations recognize sustainability issues and develop solutions.

When it comes to outreach, NGOs are not hard to find or engage. They certainly don't hide. In fact, they tend to readily call, write, and even show up to AGMs. My advice is to proactively invite them to share their concerns, then actually respond in a meaningful way.

That said, your company shouldn't wait until highly organized activist groups make noise to engage with external complaints. Numerous individual complaints typically precede such highly public responses as op-eds, white papers, or AGM demonstrations. Most companies have a complaint or inquiry email address that staff and community members can use to log concerns. As a board member, make sure complaints are getting addressed in a timely manner.

Certain sectors, like banking, are better than others at addressing complaints. Mainly because otherwise people leave online reviews to the effect of: "I went to my bank, and they were really rude, so I took my money out." Since the banking sector is so competitive, if you upset your client, they're going to withdraw their funds and move on.

Other companies may hesitate to reveal their complaints process to the board. They don't wish to admit that it takes them weeks or even months to respond to complaints. Unfortunately, when you ignore staff and community concerns, they may show up as costly turnover rates, or even very visible, memorable protests.

SUSTAINABILITY COMMITTEE

Corporate sustainability committees can do wonders for improving stakeholder engagement. This group can schedule meetings with NGOs and other community stakeholders, analyze ESG issues, and develop a sustainability plan for your organization.

While many sustainability committees meet only twice a year, I recommend quarterly meetings—at a minimum—so members stay highly engaged and develop clear timelines.

Your board's sustainability committee should include both independent board members and representatives from each department of your organization, so that everybody feels included in the sustainability plan. To be effective, the sustainability committee must be embraced as part of company culture, by everybody. It will not function properly as some perfunctory, stand-alone committee that does not represent or interact with all key internal and external stakeholders.

While this committee can be chaired by an independent board member, the CEO and the heads of all departments—or head minus one—should all be invited in. Different board committee chairs should get involved in creating a viable sustainability strategy or roadmap. You'll especially need auditing expertise and risk assessment for scenario planning, time frames, and adjustments.

What is your sustainability strategy, and where's the action plan? How are you going to adopt green technology or green innovation to reduce greenhouse gas emissions to net zero? Do you have businesses that need green certification? What is your process for ensuring supply chain sustainability? Do you have scenario planning and timelines in place for the sustainability rollout?

Above all, your plan should be evidence-based, realistic, measurable, and long-term. When you look at the 2021 UN Climate Change Conference or the Sustainable Development Goals, the resolutions and goals all include a broad time frame. Nobody says, "We'll fix this overnight and be transformed tomorrow."

Finally, it's very important for the sustainability committee to use data and metrics. You must use data to make informed decisions and plan. You do not want the sustainability committee to devolve into airy-fairy ideals with no measurable goals, a la: "I want to help the forests!"

Yes, helping forests is great—but how?

When companies have clear outcomes, informed by data and metrics, they can make more informed decisions. So, if Amazon wants to become the best employer in the world, they must meaningfully engage with stakeholders to define outcomes and measurable steps toward achieving this sustainability goal. If ExxonMobil wants to stay relevant in a rapidly changing world, they should develop a more concrete, impactful plan of allocating resources toward transitioning away from fossil fuel dependency.

The sustainability committee must define stakeholders, engage with them, and really understand what their concerns are. Does your company's operations pollute rivers, and if so, how can it stop? Is traffic safety around a school negatively impacted by your company's shipping activities? What are some safer solutions? If you should want your company to be around for a long time—and to grow—you certainly don't want the communities you work with and within to shun you.

CHIEF SUSTAINABILITY OFFICER

Many Fortune 500 companies now hire a chief sustainability officer, or CSO. Microsoft, Mastercard, Starbucks, Procter & Gamble—companies like these realize that sustainability is the only way forward for stable capital and healthy consumer relations.

I believe the chief sustainability officer should be the key person who engages with investors and other stakeholders. Publicly listed companies often have very public-facing CEOs and CFOs, as well as an investor relations director who's generally lower on the totem pole.

However, investor relations are changing. It's no longer just about taking phone calls from the investing community, then sending out a press release. Because of sustainability, stakeholder relations require an integrated, evolving strategy and action plan addressing everything from energy transition to worker relations to supply chain management.

Frankly, when it comes to ESG issues, CEOs and CFOs often have no clue. They don't even know the basics about scope one greenhouse gas emissions versus scope two. Bringing in a CSO to engage with stakeholders and inform C-suite and board decisions can make all the difference. We all know that most of what happens in the boardroom is strategy and resource allocation. Sustainability is not something to keep removed from that. In fact, it should be the lens through which you look at everything in the boardroom.

If you look at Starbucks, they've shifted to using recycled and/or recyclable materials, and they donate funds to communities they partner with. As a result, more consumers gravitate toward them. People don't mind having unbleached, brown napkins or cup sleeves to hold their coffee.

In fact, it's become fashionable to use obviously recycled materials—even literally; many fashion designers now conspicuously promote sustainable materials. Meanwhile, major jewelers advertise fair trade gold that ensures no child labor. These moves by global brands encourage competitors to follow suit.

Meanwhile, if you're a major brand dumping waste into oceans, killing turtles, whales, and other wildlife—and consumers discover you're doing nothing about it—you will get a backlash. Shareholders, NGOs, and even consumers themselves now have enormous platforms for exposing wrongdoing, taking companies to court, and demanding more oversight and accountability in business.

ADVISORY BOARDS

Whether your board approves a sustainability committee or CSO or not, it's crucial that you engage with both stakeholders and ESG subject matter experts. A lot of ESG issues get very technical, and if you don't speak to knowledgeable industry players, you'll end up with a very myopic view of what's going on and what needs to change.

One way to gain subject matter expertise is to set up an advisory board of industry experts who understand ESG issues. Unlike committees or task forces, advisory boards do not necessarily come together to discuss issues at regularly scheduled meetings. Instead, members of the advisory board may take individual meetings with the board chair or CEO, perhaps over dinner. As such, advisory boards provide direct lines to subject-specific mentors who function a bit like external legal counsel or consultants—only without such exorbitant fees.

For example, AIG maintained an amazing board of international advisors, which included the likes of Henry Kissinger. While your company does not necessarily need such high-profile advisors, it's important to tap individuals who understand sustainability in environmental, social, and governance matters—not to mention industry culture and politics.

COMMUNICATION

The worst thing you can do is either ignore or disparage shareholders, staff, community members, and other stakeholders. Board directors must realize that their company impacts every individual and community they do business with and among.

From lawsuits and critical white papers to a parade of stuffed animals covered in ketchup, you ignore shareholder concerns at your own peril. If board members and management don't proactively address issues with investors, things can get ugly—performatively and otherwise. Board members should also encourage questions from shareholders at AGMs, and provide both transparent reports and open lines of communication.

Embolden management and staff to speak up—as well as the C-suite minus one, and minus two—all the way down the line. You'll have more effective workers when you keep them engaged and listen to their ideas.

If a foreign country or faraway neighborhood hosts your factory or plantation, it's your responsibility to create a symbiotic relationship with that community. If you go into a community willing to destroy local natural resources or exploit and abuse workers, you may secure short-term gains, but your longer-term business model will fail. You will squander your resources and risk bad press, lawsuits, or worse.

As corporate leaders and board directors, we must respect our host communities and indeed all our company resources—human, natural, technological, etc. This means truly understanding all stakeholders, and communicating with them openly. Especially if there have been major conflicts in the past or there are current issues or potential emerging problems, take courage and confront these, openly and honestly. It may be uncomfortable in the short term, but you will lay the groundwork for ongoing, mutually beneficial relationships if you make foundational empathy and radical accountability part of the equation.

The most important thing is communication. Talk to people. Allocate time to meet specific stakeholders. Speak to employees or community representatives one on one. Invite them for tea or coffee just to hear them out and give them feedback.

Then, follow up and follow through.

Above all, as corporate leaders, we must abandon this idea that you've got to be tough, imposing, and locked away in some fortified boardroom tower. Staff, host communities, and consumers are not simply resources to be exploited, but rather integral parts of your company's ecosystem. NGOs and other community advocates are not your enemies, but rather your allies in understanding how your business can be more sustainable.

We are all interconnected, and as such, we all benefit from responsibility in business. When corporate leaders meaningfully respond to and engage with real issues within companies, real change becomes possible.

CONCLUSION

In spring 2020, those anxious early days of the COVID-19 pandemic, I certainly remember frantic scrambling and angry outbursts in the (mostly virtual) boardroom—but I also recall moments of inspiring and unprecedented global collaboration and care.

At the time, I was chairman of the Malaysian stock exchange in regular contact with the Shenzhen Stock Exchange. When they heard about our nation's mask shortage, they sent hundreds of masks to our office, which we distributed to frontline medical workers.

I was so touched by the profound humanity of this simple gesture. If you looked for it, you could see people helping each other like this everywhere. My sister, who works as a physician and medical academic, saw universities from different countries all over the world dropping their competitive reticence and sharing medical data, pooling both resources and research talent like never before to deal with the novel virus.

As I write this, governments, corporations, and individuals all over the world have similarly responded to the war in Ukraine: trying to help, feeling like remote stakeholders in something important—even if they're not totally sure how or even whether the events will impact them directly.

"Collaboration" is one theme of the UN's Sustainable Development Goals, and to me, it's the only way forward. In part because, when corporations, governments, and people collaborate, we all become less dependent on our individual assets and established means of production. Collaboration means communication and understanding culture. It brings innovation from concerted action on shared goals. It's far more powerful than people realize.

The pandemic forced those within corporate boardrooms—and everyone everywhere—to reassess and rebuild. It's also given us an opportunity to see how resilient and innovative we really are, and to imagine where else we might pivot.

What other things can we reassess and rebuild? For example, can we reimagine and redirect the social trajectories of our digital world?

Granted, no one doubts that "hate sells." Still, viral videos of strangers saving each other's lives (not to mention heartwarming videos of animals, babies, and family reunions) testify to the fact that hate is not the only powerful human emotion.

We have options. We can exploit baser instincts and division online, we can deplete and defile natural resources, communities, and public health—or we can innovate ways to support and leverage the very best parts of humankind.

POLITICS, CULTURE, AND ESG IN THE BOARDROOM

The dreadful ecological and social consequences of hundreds of years of an exploitation business model can no longer be ignored. Compared to previous eras, the transparency of the digital age brings new levels of accountability—and with climate change and globalization both accelerating, it's so much harder to dismiss or play dumb about environmental exploitation and social abuses.

Our deeply interconnected, swiftly warming planet has altered more than just our climate. As noted in Chapter 1, we're seeing shifts in political and cultural patterns around the world as governments, economic markets, and legal measures help regulate—and take first steps toward enforcing—ESG sustainability.

In Chapter 2, we reviewed how DEI, such as increased representation of women, on corporate boards will be a vital aspect of this necessary evolution. If you're a director or aspiring director—whether or not you hail from a traditionally underrepresented group—you can leverage both ESG knowledge and your unique perspective to join, contribute to, and improve boardroom culture.

That said, all the ESG expertise, corporate leadership experience, and good ideas in the world will not help you if you do not understand boardroom politics. Chapter 3 emphasized that progress starts with focusing on what you can offer, proper listening, and balancing the drive for change with foundational empathy for the existing corporate culture.

In Part 2, I shared what I consider to be some of the most pressing issues in environmental, social, and governance sustainability. This section filters ESG sustainability issues through my personal experiences as a Southeast Asian fund manager, CEO of an asset management group, independent director, and board chair.

I hope this unique variety of boardroom roles, diverse heritage, and intimate knowledge of emerging Asian markets provides an insightful lens on ESG matters. I've seen firsthand how the exploitation of fossil fuels destroys precious rainforests and cultures; how forced migrant labor devastates individuals, families, and communities; and how unchecked corruption leads inevitably to governance and legal reforms.

As Part 3 illustrated, I've also seen how slowly some aspects of corporate culture change—and how ugly boardroom politics can get.

When you come through those heavy boardroom doors, you can safely expect many people to say one thing and do quite another. Chapter 7 demonstrated how to smile and nod—then do your research to see what's *really* going on.

Chapter 8 explained how leadership sets the tone and influences both culture and politics in the boardroom—and offered some concrete advice for navigating committees, meeting minutes, digital communications, and more, especially as a board or committee chair.

This book ends with what I consider to be the most important topic: meaningful dialogue and engagement with all stakeholders as the primary engine of positive change and sustainable growth. And by stakeholders, I do not just mean majority shareholders and executive management, but also junior staff, consumers, migrant workers—indeed every ecosystem and community impacted by our business choices.

SUSTAINABILITY IS GOOD BUSINESS

I firmly believe that if your attitude is, "This is how we've done things for decades; better not to change," you will get left behind. Because the changing world will change you—for better or worse.

The good news? ESG sustainable business practices not only protect companies from lawsuits and regulatory fines, they also reduce operational costs. Granted, solar panels may cost more up front, but they consistently reduce costs thereafter. Ethical labor practices may be more expensive, but your labor will be better trained, and they'll stay with you longer.

When I started my own asset management firm, Corston-Smith, I wanted to focus on transparency and engage with companies to help them invest more responsibly, to support more sustainable decision-making.

Why? So we all could reap the rewards. Financial studies consistently show that ESG-minded companies consistently perform better. This leads to stronger markets with longer data capital, and a more resilient global economy able to support itself through collective crises.

As an asset management group, when we worked with companies who failed to meet our ESG standards, we didn't just dump stocks and move on, passing the problem down the line. We first tried to encourage company leaders to make changes. Could they start with a few quick wins—not greenwashing, but actual moves toward adopting ESG practices? How could they leverage those first, small steps toward a more integrated, sustainable business approach?

Sometimes we failed to inspire progress and change. Other times, companies just needed help developing a sustainability strategy and roadmap scenario plan.

Granted, when we first started advocating responsible investing in Southeast Asia in 2004, few people took interest. However, today, that small institutional investor fund we started in 2007 has grown 406 percent as of 2022, and everybody's talking about ESG. Not because they've all had some Scroogean epiphany of virtue—or even to avoid getting in trouble—but rather because they've seen that ESG sustainability yields more *stable* profits over the long term, better public relations, and lower cost of capital.

It's not just about doing and feeling good, it's also just good business.

ESG sustainability helps your company raise money and improve your branding. It allows you to add value propositions to your customers, to your stakeholders, and to your clients and consumers. As such, profitability improves. It's one big, virtuous circle.

ACCOUNTABILITY MODEL

I wrote this book to help fellow ESG-minded corporate leaders not only understand what's at stake, but also navigate changing boardroom culture and politics to help drive sustainable, ethical business growth.

Many directors underestimate the impact we can have—not only on our companies, but also on the broader economy, ecology, and affected communities. At this level of corporate decision-making, we can truly make a difference. It all starts by taking an honest account of our corporate activities and their environmental and social consequences.

I believe it's not only possible but *imperative* to move away from our exploitation model of business toward an accountability model—one in which the will of the board serves more than just the narrow financial interests of executive staff and majority shareholders.

Such ideas ought not be considered naive or extreme. They should be basic, foundational—the very roots that stabilize and nurture not only our business, but all our interconnected global systems.

We do not have to let exploitative practices continue to determine our collective fate. Global upheavals like COVID-19 show us not only the vulnerability of our interdependence, but also its strengths. Namely, how quickly and profoundly we can collaborate, adapt, and transform.

If we so choose, we can also proactively shift our boardroom culture and business model to one of radical accountability—if and when we understand how our boardroom decisions deeply impact every other business, community, ecosystem, and individual across the globe.

If and when we make it our business to build a better world.

If this book helped you and you'd like to connect or learn more, I'd love to hear from you. You can read more of my previous work at governancematters.app and ESGnomics.com.

ACKNOWLEDGMENTS

My deepest gratitude to all who made this book possible, beginning with my publishing team at Scribe Media, including—without a doubt—the editorial support of Anita Martin, invaluable feedback from Barbara Boyd, and cover design by Howard Grossman.

I'm deeply indebted to supportive individuals from the AIG family—including Mr. Maurice R. Greenberg (Hank Greenberg), Mr. Cesar Zalamea, Mr. Nonoy Colayco, Mr. Win Neuger, and Mr. Hans Danielsson—who all shared their global experiences and guided me through challenging circumstances presented by big business.

I owe so much to collaborative partners through Corston Smith-BTPS—particularly Doug Clark, an advocate for responsible investing who patiently, delicately, and consistently pushes for sustainable business practices; and Dino Bate, who always shares his own entrepreneurial experiences in the Philippines with clear support for responsible investment strategies.

I am also so thankful for top class colleagues across the industry—such as Lionel Johnson (Pacific Pension Institute), a steadfast friend providing guidance and feedback on international scenarios as they play out; Donald Kanak (formerly AIG), whose passionate commitment to green finance helps me keep faith that we can make necessary changes; Bill King (MoVi Founder) and Fred Matera (MoVi), whose positive, forward-thinking approach to responsible fintech investing and ethics has kept me focused; and Doug Pearce (formerly BCIMC), whose strong fundamental belief that responsible ESG investing is critical to ensure sustainability. I also want to thank Dan Konigsburg (Deloitte) for consistently pushing robust governance standards and diversity, as well as Carmen Niethammer (European Investment Bank) for her enormous support for my Southeast Asia 2010 Gender Diversity Research Project.

Finally, my heartfelt appreciation to my late mum, Dr. Gwendolen Daisy Smith, who gave me the confidence to write and speak up, and to my husband and three children—who remain my closest friends and definitely my toughest critics.

ABOUT THE AUTHOR

SHIREEN MUHIUDEEN is an experienced emerging markets fund manager and public board director with regulatory knowledge. She was the first female chair of the Malaysian Stock Exchange and is the former CEO of AIG Investment Corporation (Malaysia). She is an ESG (Environmental, Social, and Governance) and DEI (Diversity, Equity, and Inclusion) trailblazer, encouraging organizations to become ESG sustainable, either as an investor or as a board member. Shireen guides companies seeking to expand and raise capital in the Asia-Pacific region. She has served on investment, nomination and governance, compensation, risk, and ESG committees within banking, port, plantation, property, and media companies.

Made in the USA
Columbia, SC
25 April 2023

15488205R00126